D1132645

Discovering Senior Space

Discovering Senior Space

A Memoir

Suzanne Juhasz

ISBN: 1979008620
ISBN 13: 9781979008624
Library of Congress Control Number: 2017916541
CreateSpace Independent Publishing Platform
North Charleston, South Carolina

To My Family

Contents

Introduction

When I retired in 2007 as professor of English from the University of Colorado, Boulder, at the age of sixty-four, I set in motion my life as a senior citizen, specifically a senior woman. I retired early, for professors are not required to retire at a set time and often work well into their sixties or seventies. I did so because I didn't want to continue the life of a professional academic anymore, where I felt that I was no longer using myself to my fullest capacities. I wanted to discover what life might hold for me outside the dome under which the academy exists. Some people think of retirement as a chance to kick back a little or to spend more time on hobbies or grandchildren. But I didn't want to stop working: I just wanted to work in new ways. I had ideas about recovering dormant interests and talents and even finding ones to this point unknown. The thirty-eight-year career that had organized my life was over, as far as I was concerned, and I set out to find myself anew, just like a kid graduating from college. I didn't feel at all old, because I wasn't. "Old" in my opinion would come later. But upon retirement my life turned a corner, and I began to see that it was not so simple to discover who I was or am now. As I sought new experiences, sought to give shape to my life, the space that I had entered felt formless.

I didn't understand a thing about retirement, and I didn't understand a thing about the aging process. I thought that retirement would be like the freedom of a sabbatical term, when I got to write my book and didn't have to teach or go to committee meetings. Not so. In a sabbatical there was conclusion, going back to work at the end of the year. This was different. Cut loose from my lifelong habits, colleagues, and boundaries, I was frequently confused, anxious, and then depressed.

Plus, something more than having new experiences began to happen. Living outside of the academy made me aware as I wasn't before of my age. I wasn't old, but I wasn't middle-aged any more, either. Age didn't seem to matter when I was a full professor, but to nonacademics it seemed to define me most. I was a senior citizen.

At about the same time, my thrice-weekly ballet classes, a central aspect of my ordinary world, were abruptly terminated by the onslaught of acute arthritis and other physical problems, caused, in fact, by my long years at the barre. My body became a major player in a new and difficult way. Gone was my lifelong fluidity of movement, and though I may not have looked my age in most ways, my body now moved like an older person. Thus body as well as psyche, and their necessary congruence, changed.

Good words for this place where I have found myself might be "uncharted" or "untethered," because it is not secured by the clear guidelines of a job, a definite social position in life, and the sense of self that accompanies it. After six years of retirement (as I write), it feels as if inner and outer, mind and body, are in flux and contention, and thus my sense of identity is wobbly and under scrutiny daily.

Slowly, I started to see that many of my struggles were not only happening in but significantly defined by the space itself: senior space, aging space. I didn't understand this place, and I needed to do so. I needed to think about now—but also, I started to realize, about then: my past, my life. For what was possible now and what had happened then were not only intimately related but could be understood more fully if I could get a grasp on this place in which I had arrived. Or maybe it was the other way around. How does one create, maintain, develop, understand a self?

When I looked around me for guidelines and models, I found little to help. This was something like what had happened when my youngest child left home for college, and I was plunged into severe depression. It was in fact worsened by the world telling me how good I should be feeling, free from all that daily responsibility of childcare at last, when my heart hurt in ways that I could barely tolerate.

Now I am surrounded by media images of senior women who have little to do with me, simply because they emphasize the positive only and omit the problems. Pictures of jolly senior citizens fill the pages of the *AARP Newsletter.* "We're traveling the world!" or "I found new fulfillment in my favorite charity" or "I discovered photography." There are articles everywhere about older women who are so very successful in all professions, letting us know that increased age need not matter at all. In the pages of *Arthritis Today,* a magazine devoted to the disease with which I struggle, seniors walk briskly along a summer path with big smiles and their sweaters wrapped around their shoulders. I am delighted that now some older women film stars like Vanessa Redgrave, Helen Mirren, Angela Lansbury, Isabelle Huppert, and Shirley MacLaine have roles to play (a sign that progress is truly being made), and I applaud their spirit and achievement.

Still, all of these images give the message that aging is no big deal, that you are primarily the same as you were ten (or even twenty) years before. The *AARP Newsletter* is at the same time filled with ads for step-in bathtubs and mechanical call-for-help devices to carry at all times, but not only don't the models in the ads look like they'd ever need the devices, but no connection is made between these people and those perennially successful seniors who are the subject of the articles in the magazine. In *Arthritis Today*, despite the pages of ads for pain medications, there is no indication that the walkers ever have to take a day (or days) off because of that pain. And the stars, well, they're *stars*, with an extensive support system of makeup, personal trainers, special lighting, and so forth, to make them look so good and get them through their days so that they can appear so marvelous on stage or screen.

Finally, there are the self-help books, like Jane Pauley's *Your Life Calling*. "Find your passion," she says, "and follow it. You have the chance now." She tells many brief histories of many people, their newfound passions, and their successes in living them. If there are occasional obstacles, the people overcome them. It's one of many books that tell us: "What a time for positive change!" "You can do it!"

Yes, you can, to paraphrase Mr. Obama. But still, all of this sends the message that getting older is no big deal. And if it is for you, then *you're the one to blame*. If you must age, then do it so we can't really tell.

I'm not saying that women can't be active, happy, and fulfilled at seventy. Why shouldn't we be? Or that I myself haven't seen it as an opportunity and have in fact found much that is good during these past years. But what about the difficulties that I've mentioned, which include frustration, anxiety, loss, and even

shame? These can be part of the picture, too, and often complicate fulfillment. What about the *aging* part of aging? Aging is
real, and to pretend, as my own mother did to the bitter—very
bitter—end, that it doesn't exist is to throw a towel, as it were,
over this real and important stage of life. Even if you don't lose
desire, ambition, humor, energy, and yes, beauty, other feelings
cut across the rest in unaccustomed ways.

One path that I wanted to take in my new life was to change
the nature of my primary writing from academic studies to fiction or personal narrative. I'd always written poetry, short stories, and personal essays, too; I even started a novel during my
academic years. Some of it was published, but for the most part,
since it wasn't related to my job, I didn't try. Now, after writing
many scholarly books and essays, I wanted to bring this other
work to the fore. "No more footnotes," I'd gaily assert, but that
was just a shorthand way to say, "I want to be a different *kind* of
writer."

The writing that occurred right after my retirement was not
organized but rather short pieces. Some were about retirement
and my life now; some were about my long ago past: family,
school. Some were about the more recent past: my career as a
professor. And some were memories of my passions: acting, ballet, love. I was writing what I needed to tell myself, experiencing
these events in words. In the process, I was beginning in a hap-
hazard way to reconstruct my life: both because the present was
so difficult to understand and because I felt cut off from the past.
I began to see that what I was writing was the underpinnings of a
memoir, which ultimately became this book.

In *Discovering Senior Space*, each chapter is a different strand
of my story: specifically, explorations of the worlds of family, love,
and work. Woven together, they enable me to see who I have

been, and they offer new meanings for how I understand what has gone before. But the shape that they take also reveals something unexpected: ways in which the past is significantly implicated in my present tense. Memory itself creates a new kind of perception, as a connection between present events and earlier moments reveals itself. In such ways, I can see that this new time of instability gains unanticipated support.

This is my story, my strategy for coming to terms with the challenges of aging. I do not stand for everyone; how could I? My life is my own, shaped by many factors: the historical moment in which it has transpired, my nationality, class, race, gender, sexuality, beliefs, and especially, my feminism. My status as a second-wave feminist informs my life in powerful and long-range ways and is itself, I believe, a tale worth telling. In addition, my particular strengths and weaknesses, my needs and desires, while related to all of the above, are themselves a thread of emotional and cognitive urgency that consistently defines not only what I do but also what I think that I am doing. They bind the whole thing together.

In a small, framed photograph on my bookshelf, Suzy Hecht stares at the camera. She stands close against her grandmother, Selma Rosenthal, who wears a dark coat and a pillbox hat. Neither is smiling for the camera. Suzy is about six or seven, so the photo, black and white, must have been taken in the late 1940s. She wears a light dress that comes to her knees and has dark bangs and pigtails tied in bows. She is very serious, very intense. She looks a lot like her grandmother, I see. Where is she headed? Who will she be? The photo raises these questions, for this child is clearly thinking so hard, as she looks into the eyes of the photographer.

Now she is seventy-four, with all that life behind her (inside her), and she is still thinking so hard.

PART I

I Retire

1

Retiring: A Second Act

I am standing before a bushy-haired, bearded older man with his pen poised over the notebook on his lap. I'm wearing my best "casual" outfit: soft gray sweater and black pants. I am ready to speak my short monologue, written in verse couplets. I am sixty-seven years old and auditioning for the part of Madame Pernelle in Molière's *Tartuffe*, my first audition in fifty-three years. I know the lines; I've rehearsed. I'm ready for this. It doesn't help, though, that all the other aspirants in the room are forty years younger than I am, dressed in jeans, and they all seem to know one another. Or that I arrived too early: first, as a matter of fact. "Never mind," I tell myself. "I'm good, and I know it." After a wobbly start, I warm to my words and my character: the grand-mother—outspoken and critical. But then, to my horror, I go blank. I try again, but I don't remember anything. Shame rushes through me.

However, the director is unbelievably kind. "It's okay," he says. "Start again." I do, and I'm fine. I sail through my three minutes.

And you, his sister, seem so pure,
So shy, so innocent, and so demure.
But you know what they say about still waters.
I pity parents with secretive daughters.
Still, I am astonished when I get the part. It is my first role in
forty years.

I was an actor in my childhood and throughout college, with
a theatre major as well as one in creative writing. But when my
husband's plans for graduate school were set in motion two
years after our marriage, it became clear that I was not going to
Broadway, especially with a year-old baby. So I, too, applied to
graduate school.

But when I retired, the theatre seemed possible again. How
I wanted that intense pleasure and excitement that acting always
gave to me. I craved as well the sense of belonging that comes
in the theatre: belonging to a role, a cast, a world. I found closeness in the university world primarily with other feminists, but
that was nothing like the kind of intimacy that develops when
you are doing a show. For forty years while I was following an
academic career and raising three children, acting seemed impossible. How could I even rehearse when I was preparing for
class each night? "Anyway," I said to myself, "why would I want to
join a little community theatre? I was meant to be a real actor." I
wouldn't even go to their shows. I said it was because I just wasn't
interested in amateur theatrics, but that wasn't the true reason.
No, it was because I was jealous: I hated seeing other people up
there on the stage (unless they were professionals, but that was

different). The truth was that to touch that tender place with my mind, always, through all those many years, made my heart wrench, and I could not bear it. So I resolutely stayed away. I stayed away for forty years.

As soon as I retired, I took two acting classes. I auditioned throughout the area, and I I even appeared in several plays. But in various ways, my developing physical difficulties, coupled with the disabling effects of anxiety, including insomnia, surfaced in a more intense way than I'd experienced when I was younger. Ultimately, over a period of six years, it seemed harder to do it than not to do it. My timing was off, I think. So I paused, to see what might emerge that was possible for me.

When I was a child and then a young girl, acting was my passion. Not that I didn't have other interests. I wrote poetry from an early age. I took ballet classes. I was active in school projects. But really, it was acting from the start. At ten I directed my Girl Scout troop in Gilbert and Sullivan's *H.M.S. Pinafore,* casting myself as Sir Joseph Porter, KCB. I strutted across the stage in my nine-teenth-century officer's uniform, complete with knickers and tri-cornered hat, with my monocle and large white handkerchief and sang my heart out.

Some people become actors because they are shy and like losing themselves in another person. I was the kind who liked to perform. I didn't lose myself but became more alive as I brought a character to life. Acting fed some very different parts of that intense, emotional, "too dramatic" (people said), intelligent girl growing up in Providence, Rhode Island, in the 1950s. Not only did I love the spotlight, but the theatre satisfied my desire to belong and to live in a world that accepted me more than others that I experienced. In the casts of the plays in which I performed in school or especially the community theatre groups in Providence, I found a home. What would devastate me, again and again, was when the play was over, and back then these plays ran for just two or three days. It felt that *everything* was lost, gone, including the girl who I was in the play. Oh, the tears that I wept—until the next play came along.

Despite my intellectual prowess, I decided against going to the best high school, Classical High, because it was a four-year school. This would mean giving up the third year of Junior High and the chance to be in the senior play that occurred in the final year. Acting came first. For me that play was *Cheaper by the Dozen*, and I had the lead, playing Anne, the teenaged oldest of the twelve children, in a cute middy blouse, pleated skirt, bobby socks, and saddle shoes. At Hope High School, the less elite three-year school, I starred three years later in the senior play, Kurt Weil's 1940s musical, *Lady in the Dark*, in a bravura role that gave me three leading men, a variety of beautiful gowns, and many wonderful songs. Gertrude Lawrence, one of my idols, had played it on Broadway.

Otherwise, as a teenager I played ingenue roles in community theatres, appearing in contemporary classics such as William Inge's *Picnic* and Tennessee Williams's *The Rose Tattoo*. I was the only kid. My company rehearsed at night in a hall upstairs in a downtown building. I did my homework between scenes, and I fell in love with the leading man. He was a naval officer, for several of the men in our group came from the nearby navy station in Newport. He was, in fact, having an affair with the leading lady, who happened to be married to the director. Ah, the theatre. I should mention that his name was Dick, though that irony escaped me when I was fifteen. Both of the roles that I played, in *Picnic* and *The Rose Tattoo*, were the kid sister to the leading lady, who was in love with, of course, the leading man, a.k.a. Dick, and both of those kid sisters had crushes on the guy in the play. So no wonder.

This little imbroglio added yet more spice to a situation that was by nature so very appealing, for I loved the whole scene: the nights of rehearsing, becoming part of a tight community of dedicated people. I became friends with two of the women, a kind of little sister, I suppose, but everyone was fascinating to me in that world where I had my place. Then came the shows themselves, which we performed in a real theatre downtown for two or three performances. My scrapbook is filled with mementos of these times: photos, programs, even the handkerchief with which Dick bound a cut on my wrist in *The Rose Tattoo*. This was my alternative life: my real life, as I saw it.

I had another theatre life in those years, too. Every summer from the time that I was eleven until I was twenty-one, I went to Hillsboro Camp in Hillsboro, New Hampshire. I evolved from camper to counselor, with one year out as an apprentice in the Bar Harbor Summer Theatre, *de rigueur* for anyone who wanted to be a professional actor. When I was fifteen and still a senior camper, my best friend Chick and I discovered upon arrival day that the drama counselor had not returned that summer and that *we* were the new drama counselors! Hillsboro Camp put on a different play for each of its nine weeks. Every cabin got a turn; every age trod the boards, from nine-year-olds to teenaged CITs. They practiced every afternoon, and lo, at the end of the week, a show emerged, produced on the little stage at the end of Rec Hall, where the whole camp gathered.

There Chick and I were that day, campers ourselves, with no preparation at all for what lay before us. To put it bluntly, with no plays. Off went letters home, asking parents to find us anthologies of children's plays. Off we two went to the tiny library in the town of Hillsboro, looking for something to produce six days later. I still have literal nightmares about that library and about Chick and me, holed up in a window seat, looking through unlikely volumes for something, anything. I don't remember what the play was, but a play was produced for the camp community that weekend. And for seven more years, nine times a summer, the show went on.

Every afternoon found the two of us lying on the Ping-Pong table at the back of the Rec Hall, trying to coerce our little actors to learn their lines, to speak them so that we could hear. How we loved it! We especially loved the summer's centerpiece, the CIT/senior campers' production, usually a full-length musical, produced for Parents' Day. We were ambitious, despite the fact that our actors were always particularly busy during the days before their show, preparing the exhibit that their own activity, be it swimming or arts and crafts, would display to the parents. We produced musicals like *The Boy Friend*, *Annie Get Your Gun*, and *Peter Pan*. I remember going to the camp directors the day before *Annie Get Your Gun* was scheduled to occur—and begging them to call off the show, for we'd never even rehearsed the third act, and half of the cast did not know their lines. No way, we were told. All I know is that we put on, well, something.

I myself performed one of my all-time favorite roles in one of these shows: after all, I was the producer/director, and I could cast myself in the lead. I was Peter Pan, in green tights and a jaunty green cap with a feather. I "flew" by jumping onto the stage off the log railings that formed the sides of the stage. Then I spread my legs in their green tights, hooked my thumbs to my vest, and sang, "I gotta crow!" Imagine my thrill when, fifty years later, after finally joining Facebook, my sister and fellow camper directed me to a group for Hillsboro Camp. I announced my presence on the page, and immediately a post appeared from another former camper: "It's Peter Pan!"

Being a drama counselor was one of the best experiences of my life. A special friend and an intense theatre life satisfied central needs for my happiness.

When the time came for college, I chose to apply to schools that emphasized art and creative work, and ultimately I went to Bennington. There I did a double major in theatre and creative writing. I played parts as diverse as Martirio, the humpbacked spinster, in Frederico Garcia Lorca's *The House of Bernarda Alba* and the saucy Dulcie in Sandy Wilson's musical *The Boy Friend.* But there I had my first experience of not always getting the parts that I wanted, cause for days of grief. This, I confess, contributed to my secret worry about the next step, Broadway. That was where one became a professional actor. Beyond that notion, my plans for what would happen or even how I would get there were completely vague.

For I was planning to be married three days after my college graduation. I was deeply in love with my first real boyfriend. When we met, he was a nineteen-year-old freshman at Brown, I a fifteen-year-old high school sophomore. As a staunch believer in true love (I was, after all, a lifelong novel reader), I decided that he was the one, and so he stayed the one for five years until first he and then I graduated. After my graduation, we were off to Norfolk, Virginia, where he was a naval officer repaying his full navy scholarship to college, and I became, of all things, a navy wife. In this way, my plans for Broadway dissolved into the air—especially when, to my surprise and shock, I found myself immediately pregnant. For two years I lived the strange life of housewife and mother, all by myself in a tiny apartment far from home. I stood before my vacuum cleaner or folding diapers and cried, "I went to Bennington for this?" When my husband applied to graduate school, so did I. It wasn't a foolish decision: I loved to read; I loved to study literature. Plus, it was school: a place that I had known all of my life and where I'd always excelled. Besides, what else was there for me to do?

There was one last play before my acting life vanished. Joseph's ship went for a two-month deployment to South America, and I went home to Providence with my six-month old baby girl, Alexandra. This was just time enough to audition for the part of Sonja in Chekhov's *Uncle Vanya*, to be presented by the fledgling company, Trinity Square Playhouse, now one of the nation's leading regional theatres. I got the part, and with a built-in babysitter, my mother, I was able to rehearse for a month and then perform for four nights a week the following month. I was actually in repertory! Two of the actors and the director were professionals from New York; the rest were local people. This was practically the real thing. A great play, a fine cast, and a splendid role. And once more that little community, getting closer all the time during a month of rehearsal followed by a month-long run of the show.

Then it was over. The last performance, the cast party, and the next day Joe, who'd made it back for the final weekend, Suzy, and Alexandra returned to Norfolk in the morning. Back in my apartment, dusting and cooking, walking the baby in her stroller, my husband aboard the ship all day and some nights, I mourned. Sonja was gone and the play with her. Who was I here in Norfolk anyway? Not myself, that was for sure. Where was the actor? Where, indeed, was the poet who had written a novel in verse for her senior thesis? I hadn't written a poem since Alexandra was born. In graduate school, I reasoned, I could at least write poetry again, I hoped. As for the theatre: that aspiration had to be put on the shelf. Later.

When I retired, the theatre seemed possible again. Now was the time to try again. But how? Then my daughter Jenny read in the paper that a local group called Theatre 13 was giving classes for adults, and the idea seemed promising. Maybe a class would be a good way to begin, and I certainly had no intention of taking one at the University of Colorado. We went to see a production by this company in a little theatre up in the attic of the Boulder Art Museum, and it was good. Two days later, fearfully but with determination, I signed up for their class.

The instructor, Michael French, was a funny, sweet Black British man with a charming accent and a huge smile. The other students were adults, ranging in age from the twenties to sixties (me): students, teachers, lawyers, and one retired person. All wanted the experience of acting: some for the first time, some from the experience of it. From the very first class—an introductory talk by Michael, warm-up exercises, some improvisation—the feeling of having arrived surged inside me.

Michael was a wonderful teacher: intense, involved, and creative. When we were working, he would be drawn physically closer and closer to the actors, until he was squatting down close to the floor before us, every element of his being engaged and his eyes alight with attention. To be the object of that energy and concern made me feel so alive, eager to be the best that was in me. Every exercise was at the same time happily familiar and challenging. The class itself, those disparate people, grew close in that theatre way until we belonged to each other: a group. Especially when we started working on two-person short plays, which we eventually performed in a little showcase. Then the scene partner became an intimate. When I told my partner, who was actually an established actor, about my joy in acting again, she said simply, "You've come home."

Thereafter I threw myself into the theatre world of Boulder with all the focus and energy that I could muster. I took another inspiring class from Chris Thatcher, who taught the Meisner Method. I learned something crucial: that acting wasn't about me at all! I had always been a good actor, knowing how to find myself in someone else and, using this springboard, how to be that person. But always a part of me was there as well, watching herself: "How am I doing?" But Meisner taught me how to listen, really listen, to the other actor, to react only to what I heard and saw—all of which gave me no time for watching myself, something that of course pulled me *out* of the character. Only then, in my sixties, did I become a really good actor. In my second act.

I did auditions around the area and actually performed in six plays. In these ways, my acting life returned. I was rehearsing and performing, in classes or in plays, and I was an adult now, with a deeper understanding of myself and others to help me improve my skills.

When I was a teacher, people frequently would ask me, "Isn't teaching a form of acting?"

"No," I would answer. It's performing, yes, but performing an orchestrated version of oneself. Acting is something else. You have to know when you enter or exit and where you're meant to move on the stage; you speak words not your own that you've memorized. You take a curtain call. But in my opinion, these things are secondary to the central part of the experience. As Sanford Meisner said, "Acting is truth in imaginary circumstances."

I wanted to do it for real: in a play on a stage with a real audience. Astonishingly, I lucked out at my first audition. "The Upstart Crow" is a little company that has been around for a long time, producing Shakespeare and other classics. I auditioned for Madame Pernelle in Moliere's *Tartuffe*—and I got the part!

True, there was only one other person auditioning for it, but still. Afterward, I had a drink with the other cast and crew downstairs. I let it be known that it was my first part since 1964—and that I was thrilled. I was babbling. I went home on the proverbial cloud nine.

Right off the bat, however, something that had been a small problem sometimes in acting class became a big one: I had enormous difficulty memorizing, especially for this play. With its rhyming couplets, you couldn't ad lib! I was dumbfounded. I'd always been a whiz at memorization. I found out later that with age the ability to memorize decreases; older actors are the bane of directors. Ultimately, I learned to make up for my deficit by simply working much harder than anyone else.

In *Tartuffe*, my difficulty scared me to death, no matter that I finally did learn the lines. I'd forget them anyway when I was on stage, especially when someone I knew was in the audience, which made me even more anxious. I'd just go blank. Each performance was a challenge. But I solved it by making use of a talent that I did have. Not only was I an English professor, excessively familiar with poetry, but I also had written my share of comic poems, generally in rhymed couplets. So, because I knew the point of what I was to say, or often got one of the lines right, I could make up another line that would fit, right on the spot. The cast, many of whom were on stage in my big scene, made a game of it: to see what I would come up with this time.

I loved my lavender gown and silver wig with ringlets. I loved the long corset bra that gave me a tiny bit of cleavage. I even loved sitting around and gossiping in the green room with some of the other actors when I wasn't on stage. I had done it: I was an actor again.

Later I learned more about this company, after I'd auditioned unsuccessfully for several more roles for two years. The older women were almost always played by the director's first wife *or* by his second wife, the leading lady was his daughter, and old friends filled the ranks. It's really a reparatory company, with only the small roles available for others. I played one tiny role in *Lady Windermere's Fan* to show my goodwill, but I finally gave up with them.

As I progressed in my quest, I learned much more about local theatre. Only one other company in town did well, operating on a semiprofessional level. I auditioned for them several times, and once I even made a call back, as we say. But it turned out that they had a favorite older woman, too. Other small companies simply didn't tend to last. Each of the neighboring towns had a community theatre. I auditioned at all of them. They too had their resident older lady.

I delighted in the roles that I did get, no matter how marginal the shows. I had two parts (one a young woman from India!) in a set of three one-act plays at the summer Fringe Festival. I had a wonderful monologue in *The Vagina Monologues* with a director who made the now-classic series of monologues into a play with music and movement.

Then I had the opportunity to become involved in a new company in Boulder just starting up, Theatre O. For a year I helped to create the theatre: figured out our mission statement, sent out publicity announcements and calls for donations. I even shopped for groceries for the director. But when we finally produced a show, I wasn't cast. I heard later that the director just didn't like me. Soon afterwards, the company folded.

These are some of my tales. They are hardly unusual. Rejection is the name of the game in theatre, and I knew that. I understood that I wouldn't simply take the Boulder theatre world by storm, no matter how good I was. But gradually I grew alert to other factors in this endeavor, issues that I hadn't seen at the start or didn't want to see.

For one thing, starting all over like a twenty-year-old, willing to be rebuffed again and again, to kowtow to anyone in power to get ahead wasn't so easy for me as an older person with a high-powered career behind me. I'd already done all that in another lifetime. Then there was the driving. I'd always hated to drive, and the older I got, the worse it became. Initially I'd simply ignored the fact that what I was trying to do would involve doing half-hour commutes beyond Boulder proper to the neighboring towns on a nightly basis, often in foul weather. But after the initial excitement wore off, along with the desire to get a role at any price, the reality came home. I was frightened by so much driving. More importantly, there was the high-anxiety level that accompanied auditions and even performances, especially because of the memorization issue. My lifelong battle with insomnia flared. The more I didn't sleep, the more I worried about driving to the theatre, and the more I dropped my lines when I was appearing in a show. It didn't get better, even after I'd done auditions and appeared in some plays. Even when the weekly class rolled around, I didn't sleep much the night before or the night of class, so despite my devotion to those three hours, they were taking their toll.

Finally, there was the onslaught of my arthritis, which occurred just as my theatrical ambitions soared. Hip, knee, neck, ankle. The gradually eroding disk in my lumbar spine. The ankle that kept spraining. Impossible to sit on folding metal chairs. Saying, "No, I can't help build the risers in the new theatre." Not being able to handle all those stairs to get to the rehearsal space at Upstart Crow. Even the inability to do all of the physical exercises that are a part of preparation in acting class. Apologizing, apologizing. "I'm sorry but—." Or pretending that it didn't hurt so I could be like everyone else.

In these ways, age crept upon me. At first I looked fiftysomething, and no one suspected that I was sixtysomething. Not even me. But ultimately I began to understand the truth: age matters. Not just because there are much fewer roles available to me, but because situations and conditions that would not bother a younger person bothered me a lot. I felt such guilt. Why wasn't I tough enough, when I'd been throughout my life? Never give up: that's my motto. It always worked before. It came as a shock when this time it didn't.

Finally, I took stock—and slowed down. I stopped auditioning. And regretfully, after another year, I stopped going to class. I didn't think that I'd exactly given up. I was ready for something that might turn up. What, I didn't really know.

I missed it; of course I did. No more challenge, excitement, fullness, or joy. (Or even misery, when the show does not go well or you don't get the part.) The very intensity of the emotional life. When the age-old thirst for the theatre was slaked for those few years, I felt life pulsing through me in that familiar and fulfilling way. But I had to put my desire in a drawer, like Peter Pan's shadow: it remained a part of me, just not in view. My expectation was dashed by present circumstances. It was hard, very hard, to learn that one is so vulnerable to time, that not only the body but also the ingredients of personhood itself undergo sea changes so that what was manageable worry could now get in the way of my desires. It seemed that had started back too late.

Then a year later, I found out about a senior theatre group in Boulder called VIVA. "Aha," I thought. Senior! Me! I went to a few meetings, to discover that they mostly did skits for one another and an occasional short play written by a local person at the library theatre. But they did have ambitions for more, and that very spring they were going to try a series of short plays in a real theatre. There would even be auditions. I couldn't sleep the night before the auditions, but I went, hoping that adrenaline would get me through. I was the only non-VIVA member there—it was a tight group. But I was counting on my talent to get me in the door.

We were given synopses of the plays, so I tried to choose the ones that I could do physically. Not, for example, the play where a woman throws herself on the floor! After I read for the play that takes place on an airplane, with two seated passengers and a stewardess, I became concerned about the stewardess role: pushing a heavy cart, for example, so I put a note on my audition sheet to the effect that I had a bad back and that maybe this play might be a problem.

A few days later came a phone call. It was the director of the airplane play, and he was offering me the part—of course—of the stewardess! I was so happy to have a role, but I had to be upfront: "I do have a bad back, so I hope we can accommodate."

"Sure," he said. That was in February, right after my fall, but I figured I'd be okay by the time we began rehearsing in April. The plays would be presented in late May.

My house became the place to rehearse, for it was central for the other participants: two more actors and a director, Jim. He was an old hand, having done regional for years. His white or yellow golf sweaters were signs of his passion for the sport. He was in his eighties, he told me, but he'd had his knee replacement and was now "fit as a fiddle." The other actors were the passengers. One was a pretty young girl only recently graduated from college. She didn't belong in a senior group, I thought, but the director had worked with her before, and he wanted her for the part. The other woman was in her sixties, slim and attractive, and a hard worker who wanted to make things perfect. She arrived at the first rehearsal having already charted her part into miniscule moments.

When we rehearsed, Jim began with a lecture on acting: clearly, he didn't consider that we knew anything. Yet he himself was mostly concerned with how we put the stress on certain words ("This is comedy," he'd say); with the blocking and timing of my actions: offering drinks, headsets, pillows. Relating to one another was not on his agenda. I sighed. The whole setup was a little strange, but this was what I wanted, a play.

Fast forward to Sunday, May 5. After rehearsing weekly since the beginning of April, after the painful work of learning lines, and after a gala fundraiser party (so much pleasure to have that belonging feeling: I was a cast member now), the director called me one day—and fired me! He was worried, he said, that my physical problems might impede the production, and he had to think first of his show. No, my performance wasn't an issue, he said: it was my unpredictability.

What had I done? He didn't know about my struggle to repeat and repeat, as one does in rehearsal, physical movements that were a strain for me but not dangerous. I asked for accommodations only when I felt that they were necessary. I thought that I was safe doing this, because after all, I'd laid out the territory from the start. ("I do have a bad back, so I hope we can accommodate." "Sure.") And because, after all, it was a *senior* theatre group. Surely other VIVA members had their limitations and impediments, and this would be a common situation. True, the other actors in my play were younger, but the director wasn't, not at all. I was the only one in my play to mention such matters. (I had no idea what was happening with the other plays, for they were being rehearsed separately.) But this was my play, my director, and my problem.

No, I couldn't pull a cart down the aisle behind me, but yes, I could push a cart forward, if it weren't too heavy. But he wanted everything literal and realistic, so the idea of creating something a little smaller than usual was beyond his scope. He was upset when I suggested that I might wear running shoes on my feet to give me the real support that I need. Then it turned out that the only night to for us to meet at the actual theatre space—unplanned but suddenly available—was the day when a spring blizzard was forecast. (Why were we getting only one chance to rehearse in the theatre? Why was it unscheduled? We didn't even have a cart yet. This was a very amateur group, but I was the beggar who couldn't choose.) Nonetheless, I had to tell them that walking on new ice would too dangerous for me with my bad hip and ankle. There was no understanding of this problem. The blizzard arrived, the others met, and I didn't go. To me one rehearsal wasn't worth falling and breaking a hip. Was I out of line? Should I have kept my mouth shut and followed orders? From their point of view, *yes*.

Fired! I'd never been fired from anything ever. I was astonished, disheartened, and deeply depressed. A few days later, I began to understand that for him I really was a problem. I may have been the best actor, the only one with training. But he didn't want a problem. So a mere two weeks before the show opened, he decided to find another actor.

Being fired from this totally amateur production was the last straw. I'd thought all along that I was doing Theatre Lite, but that was where I belonged now. I wanted to act, so I did it. Of course there are plenty of plays with less physical roles, but this had happened now, and I was humiliated. For me VIVA had seemed my last resort, and even they probably wouldn't cast me again.

It really was time now. I'd had some lovely experiences, but it wouldn't work to try so hard against odds that I couldn't control. For I was my own worst enemy—or time was, which is after all the space in which a person lives. Acting was over for me: a dream that I had to relinquish.

2

Reverence: Retiring from Ballet

"Reverence" is a French term from the vocabulary of classical ballet. Students face the teacher at the end of class, and all perform a brief series of steps that end in a curtsy or bow to one another and to the pianist, thereby acknowledging and showing respect for them. In English, the word has meanings that include respect, honor, and even awe. I feel reverence for ballet, along with other strong emotions: joy, challenge, and dedication.

My last "reverence" in a ballet class took place when I was sixty-six, after a lifetime of taking classes.

Ballet wasn't one of my new goals for retirement: it was a part of my life. I was never what I call a "real" dancer, never good enough for that, and never even wanting it. I liked taking class. Once a week when I was a child and a young adult had become three times a week from my forties on. This activity was my major form of exercise. But it was much more than that. It was an avocation, an art form that allowed me to experience myself in a physical form. Always in the background of my life of work and family, ballet was nonetheless an underpinning to it.

When I was a child, ballet was Miss Simpson's class up a flight of stairs in downtown Providence: a bus ride with my cousin Judy, pink tights and short-sleeved black leotard, and the whack of a cane against the back of a knee that wasn't straight enough. Then came Martha Wittman, the beautiful, willowy teacher at Bennington, where there was one ballet class only, because Bennington was internationally renowned for modern dance. I, however, preferred the beauty and power of arabesques and battements to the "self-expression" of going across the floor and pretending that I was a leaf blown by the wind.

When I moved to Boulder in the '70s, I went to the studio above the local tavern, but the teacher scared me. Barbara Demaree is still, in her eighties, one of the loveliest women and finest teachers that I know, now that I know her. But then I fled. Her class seemed too difficult, too intimidating, when I attended just that once. At that time, my ten-year-old daughter Jenny was taking gymnastics, so I joined a group of adults, mostly parents, to see what her sport was all about. I wasn't bad at it, and I truly enjoyed going out for drinks with everyone afterward, but it was hurling myself at things and trying not to fall off things that made me yearn for ballet.

So at forty I began ballet class again. I put myself in a situation that I rarely entertain: not being the best, always my goal in life. For by then I knew that the dancing itself mattered more. I continued until I was sixty-five.

But then, so suddenly, it was just—over. One day I sat down at my desk chair and somehow slid onto the wooden floor of my study, so gently it seemed. But afterward there was pain everywhere: my back, hip, knees, neck, and ankle. It turned out that all those familiar movements that were the stuff of ballet—those repetitive movements that made me strong and agile and graceful, were also wearing down my bones and tendons and ligaments. I was diagnosed with severe arthritis. "No more ballet class for you," said the doctor. I have never been back.

These parts of my body had actually been bothering me on and off in class for a while, but everything always calmed down, then mended. In the ballet world, something is always hurting, and early on you are taught the mantra: "Dance through the pain." I knew how to modify the steps to suit my needs. When my back hurt, I didn't do backbends. When my ankle sprained, I didn't jump. But there was so much that I could always do, and though I would laugh and say, "Of course one day I will have to stop," I couldn't really imagine it.

I needed ballet. Whatever else was happening to me—a divorce, a promotion, a daughter's wedding, a grandchild's birth, and even my retirement—it was always there. Every week, unless I was very sick or the weather was very bad, I went to class. In its own and different way, ballet class was like my writing: a peg on which I hung my sense of self. I have been a scholar, a teacher, a writer, and a reader, living for the most part in a whorl of words. But I found in dancing a different kind of language. It is one that I speak when my body moves in space. I think of this as another form of identity, a corporeal self.

My grief about this is great. Tears still thicken my voice when I speak about it. Why not, when my life has undergone a surgery? When my body itself has suddenly become strange and new? It is so shocking to me that I have spoken much about this, although people think that talking about "aches and pains" is impolite. But I have been a dancer, a member of a world that is preoccupied with the physical body, which is the dancer's instrument, after all. We love our bodies, we tend our bodies, and we never really believe that our bodies will abandon us.

As an amateur dancer, I did not live as professionals do: class in the morning, rehearsal in the afternoon, and performance at night. The careers of real dancers tend to end at about forty, if the extreme overuse of their bodies hasn't grounded them before. By then, most professionals have had their hip replacement and their ankle surgery. The toll of this demanding art on the body is enormous, even as its rewards are equally great, and the sites of injury were the same for me as for real dancers. The difference is, as I have been saying in a determinedly light voice, "I did not perform, so I got twenty-five more years."

But I did make a life that held space for that corporeal self to grow and thrive. My loss is great, for ballet was so much more for me than an exercise routine. For one thing, it was a small society, a world, in which I lived. Perhaps most importantly, because of the nature of this art, to study it was something akin to a practice.

Most people, when they go the ballet, see the end result only. And it is not entirely a cliché to say that when the dancer does it well, the audience doesn't notice how hard it is, only how beautiful. (That's why I hate it when they clap upon seeing a turn or jump that looks difficult: this is not a circus that they're watching.) Only through extended study does a person participate in the practice to which I refer.

The ballet class is a set formation of exercises with which we learn and hone technique. Ballet is not modern dance. It is not focused on "self-expression," and there are a finite number of steps in its repertoire. In class we do these steps over and over in different combinations, always in the same order: barre, center, tendue, adagio, small jumps, then big jumps: a developmental succession of movements to train both muscles and mind in an organized pattern. A teacher can and always does change the arrangement of movements in which the primary step is presented, and teachers have their own ballet styles, the manner in which they do the steps, so there is always something new to learn, to do. I have taken ballet classes all over the country. My teachers have been American, Austrian, Chinese, Australian, Russian, and Brazilian. They have used different styles—Balanchine, Vaganova, Bourneville, Cecchetti—but the steps are the same. Thus we experience both sameness and difference in a fluid arrangement. No class is the same, and all classes are the same. The repetition is important, for in this way a system of movement is installed in the dancer's body as a way to move and work.

Take the plié, for example, the first exercise at the barre. With pliés you start to enter ballet in your body, in your mind. Pliés are a kind of meditation for me. As I bend my knees and legs and stretch my body forward and down or backward or from side to side, I feel my outside life slipping off me like a garment. I start to become my body. Doing pliés, we progress through the positions, from first position to second, maybe fourth, then fifth, establishing all the centers from which the body will then move. The combination of steps is not difficult; it doesn't require much in the way of concentration on their sequence, so there is all the time in the world (it feels as if the world has just blossomed into this space only, a very large space, really) to think about not just the placement of the muscles and the bones but how they feel inside me, how they pull and turn and firm themselves, and there is joy in knowing how fully they are present and willing to work.

My mind tunnels in and then out again through my fingers and feet, so that I start to see the world from this body that I am.

As class progresses, following its traditional order, the steps grow more and more active and difficult. My own engagement, concentration, and effort increase, as I give myself over to ballet space and time.

Ballet is hard. Not only because the steps are difficult to do but because they are meant to be done perfectly. And perfection is always out of reach. Maybe, for me, this is exactly the right, albeit paradoxical, situation. In ballet my natural inclination to work and to strive brings me into contact with a route that transpires through the body rather than the intellect, thus expanding or perhaps finding a mode of expression that supplements in powerful ways my usual manner of knowing, and giving of, myself.

For me, not any kind of dance will do. Ballet is the form that suits. It is the most rigorous, the most beautiful—both to see and to feel—and the most formal. Every movement made by every part of the body has the correct procedure and shape. You cannot cheat in ballet. You must do it right and then go beyond so that it becomes art. You find your freedom and expressiveness in patterns that are already established. Some people have chafed at what they felt to be ballet's restriction and rigidity. This is how modern dance was born. But I think that you get something special *because* of the rules. First, you participate in a ceremony that has been happening for centuries. The choreographer or teacher contributes her or his own spin (as it were) on the steps; the dancer gives her or his own unique body and soul to the choreography. It is always new, but it is at the same time always part of a greater, ongoing dance. Second, the dominance of the forms themselves, the lexicon of steps, provides a framework that

I see as especially configured for the meeting of music and body, a set of shapes particularly suited to the corporeal manifestation of the human spirit.

This is why ballet is so difficult. For the movement to work, you should have every part of your body in exactly the correct position. You can never make do, never slough off, or you will not find the required shape. When things don't quite work—which is most of the time—you know it. Something is out of kilter. You aren't all the way *there*. But when it does work, if only for a moment, you feel a sense of wholeness and integrity that is like nothing else. You inhabit space in exactly the right way, and your self is released into the movement, revealed by the movement. Amazing. And then you move on, to try again with different steps.

Although I was never really good, I am proud to say that I was a better dancer at fifty and sixty than I was at twenty or thirty. Better means a lot. Especially because, notwithstanding the endless pressure every minute of every class to do it right, everybody there knew that you could never do it right, only better. Along with its discipline, and of course its beauty, I loved ballet's challenge, the gauntlet thrown down to try *that hard*. Hence, a practice. An art.

Class meant for me as well a small society to which I belonged, now cut out of my life. I would walk into the studio, pull my warm-up pants over my tights, don my soft pink shoes, and enter the classroom. The rumbles from construction work outside the window or even the daily weather mattered little to the life that was lived there. All around me were other students stretching. Some sat on the floor while some leaned against the wooden barre surrounding the room, all wearing the motley assortment of sweatpants, tee shirts, and knit leggings over leotards and tights that comprise warm-up gear. Some were very quiet and intent on their own movements; others gossiped softly, as they leaned over a leg or curved a back.

Of course, there were always the real dancers, supple and strong, with the long legs and small heads requisite for professionals. Maybe they were on their way to a career; maybe they already had one and for some reason found themselves in Boulder, Colorado, for a while. They were the ones upon whom the teacher would concentrate.

But there were as well the amateurs, many of whom were middle-aged and even older, like me: just as devoted, if not as accomplished. If any of my pals were in class, I'd gossip with them. I knew them all: the ones who stayed and stayed and the ones who were there for a few years and then faded away. Some of the older ones, but younger than me, gave out because of an injury, but I never gave a thought to that ever happening to me.

I never saw most of these people out of the studio. (I used to joke, if I ran into someone at the market, "Oh, I'm not used to seeing you with your clothes on!") But I knew their stories, and they knew mine. Our concern for one another was warm and real. Despite our many other differences in life situation and age, for an "older" dancer can be thirty-five or sixty, we shared something deeper: our love for ballet. Our most intense bond came when the class began, and our bodies moved side by side, as we gave our hearts over to the art that is ballet.

In class there are the students, but most importantly, there is the teacher. The teacher runs the show and is at the center of every pair of eyes: revered, feared, and even resented—all of above. A class has its meaning because of what the teacher does and says. Mostly, comments and criticism or praise are directed to the class as a whole. Sometimes an individual student is singled out for a correction. This is always an honor, even if the correction is negative. You learn from that; it is a personal assessment of your work.

I adored my most recent teacher, Robert Sher-Machherndl, with his Euro-chic style, his long thin body and shaved head, his pride and ambition to do world-class work in our small university town. He is Austrian, has danced all over Europe, and moved to Boulder after marrying a woman who lives here. His own choreography is a kind of funky contemporary ballet, with dancers on pointe but no tights. But he knows and teaches the classical style with respect and intense energy. That energy, the athleticism of his movements, was what drew me the most.

And I always think with love of my favorite teacher, Barbara Demeree, with whom I studied for many years. She has retired and returned so many times, so skilled and beloved is she, and still in her eighties, she is teaching. She is British and once danced at what was then Sadler's Wells, now the Royal Ballet. Her movements are graceful and elegant; plus she is one of the best *teachers* that I've ever known. She understands that praise for the one thing that a student can do well, despite all the other things that that person cannot do, does more for that student than all the criticism combined (albeit "corrections" are important, too). I always tried to remember to do this in my own classroom.

This was a world in which I lived for so long, but now it has ended for me. My basket of leotards and tights is still where it was on the day when I was told that I could not go back. I can't throw them out, despite the fact that I now have a life in which they will never be used again. Arthritis is a disease that cannot be cured. But it can be controlled. I am told that I must move, move, move to keep it from growing worse, but I am forbidden to move, move, move in a ballet class, for that is dangerous for my body.

I cannot, in fact, move spontaneously anymore. I, whose stance in the world has always been characterized by fluidity, must take care and think about where and how I step or place my arms. I often feel that I am no longer in my own body, but nevertheless I have to care for this new one.

I take therapeutic Pilates sessions twice a week, and this form of exercise (invented by a dancer) is both pleasurable to me and life-enhancing. It keeps me strong and supple, and I am blessed to have an exceptionally skillful instructor. I walk, and I ride the recumbent bike. I enjoy the deep blue autumn sky as I walk and the calm that the repetition of cycling brings. All of this helps my disease. But in the end, this body wants to dance.

I was just watching a recent film about a dancer who had defected to the United States from Communist China. There was a scene, a very minor moment, really, when the company director is teaching a duet to the dancer and his partner for the first time. The director simply calls out the steps to them: glissade, pas de beurré, changement, and the dancers do them. I gasped, as if something had pierced me. "Oh," I thought, "I will never hear that again, never do that again."

But there is more to the story, it turns out: a sequel. For my granddaughter, now seventeen, is a student at Houston Ballet, training to be a professional ballet dancer.

I brought her to her first movement classes when she was five. I sat with the mothers to watch, each year until it was time for beginning ballet classes. I watched that small strong body and how she always had the tempo right and picked up the steps so much more easily than the other children. She was so determined and focused, whereas most were far from that. She struggled with piqué turns, which she hated, over and over, until one day she succeeded. You can say that I was prejudiced: I am her grandmother, but I knew.

I kept watching, even after the mothers felt that their kids were old enough to be left alone and just dropped them off. I saw her skill grow, along with her joy. But then, one day when she was eight, she stood outside the car as I was ready to drive her to class, stomped her feet, and burst into angry tears. She called for her mother. "I don't want Grammy to take me to class anymore," she cried. "I hate it. She is always looking at me!" And so I was banished from her classes.

That was fair, I really did know, no matter how sad I felt. She was claiming ballet for herself.

Soon after, she began to perform in her school's yearly Nutcracker Ballet, and I was now an audience member. When she was only eleven, she starred as the little girl Clara, with ringlets in her hair and a white party dress. In the opening party scene, her shining smile and skillful movements focused our attention. But it was later in the act, when Drosselmeyer the magician lifted her high in the air as they danced together before the six-foot-high Christmas tree and she almost flew above him like a brilliant star herself, that I saw something more. For the stage belonged to her: it comes alive when she is present, for she is so vital and glowing. Tiny and slim in body, she is big in heart and spirit. Now she has given her heart to ballet. And my own heart expands when I watch her dance.

Soon she was chosen for summer workshops at top ballet companies, and then, last year, when she was fifteen, Houston Ballet invited her to be a student in their all-year school. This is an honor and a challenge. Students study ballet all day—and do their high school homework at night and on weekends. So begins the traditional path toward a professional career. I am still watching—as the little girl learning to point her toes properly grows into a lovely, confident, skillful young woman. A dancer.

Maybe I've passed something on to her somewhere in the genes, but more likely I simply shared with her my own love of this demanding, rewarding art. My own loss still hurts, and that will never leave me, but ballet is not gone from my life. These days Eliza and I talk ballet with one another, and through our relationship, I experience it in a new way. Yesterday Eliza, her mother, and I were having lunch and discussing her summer plans. "I like to hear what Grammy thinks," she said. "She knows a lot." She is my heritage now, and that is real. Not everything, no, but a great gift.

3

Retiring in a New Voice

Senior aging. The changes that it rings, the challenges that it poses. Along with loss has come something new, reminding me that there is possibility in this space as well.

I have learned how to sing. It came in through the back door, so to speak. I've always loved to sing: walking across campus or in the proverbial shower. Indeed, I sang in high school and college musicals. My voice, however, was never trained. So in the early days of my retirement, I decided to take lessons to audition properly for musical theatre. My granddaughter Emma, Eliza's older sister, had been appearing in musicals since she was a little girl. I went to the woman who'd been Emma's teacher from the time she was ten. I liked my lessons. It turned out to be hard work, a skill that I lacked completely. But I liked the effort. Early on in my studies, I even auditioned for the chorus in *Brigadoon*—before I understood that I could not do the dancing! What a jolt: the aspect of musicals that I thought I had aced.

With the lessons came an unexpected gift: the opportunity to sing all of my favorite songs in a new way. For learning required that I choose what to sing, and I found myself wanting the old songs, the ones that I had loved since I was young. I have discovered that my treasure box is deep. As a girl I would lie on the living room rug and listen to records. It was the 1950s—vinyl. There were *my* records, to which I listened publicly, and my mother's records, which I devoured in secret, when she wasn't home. Mine were folk music, the Weavers, Pete Seeger, and even older songs, ballads of the British Isles, sung by Alfred Dyer-Bennett. There was Gilbert and Sullivan. All the musicals of the 1940s and 1950s: Cole Porter, Rogers and Hammerstein, Rogers and Hart, and Lerner and Lowe. And there were my favorites of all, "Noël and Gertie," the affectionate term for Noël Coward and Gertrude Lawrence. I knew the words to all of their songs by heart. My mother was in love with Frank Sinatra, but I was in love with Noël Coward. My passion for him tells a lot about my deeper desires: the wit, the sophistication, the romanticism tinged with irony. I read and listened to everything of his that I could find. "Someday I'll Find You," the theme song from his enduringly beloved play, *Private Lives*, sung by his favorite leading lady, Gertrude Lawrence, was my favorite song of all, and it was the first song that I asked to sing in my voice class.

My mother liked "Frankie," Ella Fitzgerald, Louis Armstrong, Judy Garland. I thought that they were too ordinary, too popular (I was a teenage snob), but I listened to all of them, anyway. Once as an adult, when I visited my mother, I asked if I could bring home to Boulder—just to borrow, I said—her Ella and Louis album. I also wanted Ella singing *The Rogers and Hart Songbook*, plus *The Cole Porter Songbook*.

Now all of this music has been opened to me again, Judy Garland as well as Noël Coward. *Judy Garland at Carnegie Hall*—joy. Now I study these songs and find the intricacies in music as well as lyrics. And now I sing them! Shockingly, I discovered that with training I am not an alto, as I'd always believed, but a mezzo-soprano. I can even sing the ballads written for the heroines of those cherished musicals, for I have created a way of making these lyrics that belong to twenty-year-olds work for me, by adding a dose of irony (learned from who else but Noël). "The hills are alive with the sound of music," sang my sentimental unfavorite Julie Andrews, and so do I.

My teacher Dorinda Dercar is not much younger than I am: a clever, determined, tough, funny survivor who can juggle more balls in a day than anyone I know. We have to stop telling each other stories so we can get to work, but we do both, and I have made a friend as well as gained a talented and creative teacher.

Two years ago, Dorinda and I imagined creating a group of singing women, and through her contacts in the music world, she made it happen. Five women, ranging in age from the late forties to sixties to me, seventy, plus a wonderful accompanist, Robyn, in her fifties, gathered once a week. I was the only newbie, as I call myself: they were all, or were, professional singers in one form or another. We operated according to what I understand to be a customary format: each person sang for the others with a mike, usually two songs a meeting, and the rest of the group listened, commented, and enjoyed. Usually I chose one that I'd sung the week before to work on it further. But our custom was that the other be a new one. In this way my "repertoire" expanded ex-ponentially. I worked on the songs in my weekly lesson, so I was somewhat ready for my turn when the group met, but not nearly as much as I'd like to have been. When I went up to the little stage, it was a leap of faith. This turned out to be good for me: I couldn't rely on my preparation as a shield to make me safe, as I'd learned to do in other arenas of my life. Frightened as I was, I simply had to get up and try.

In response, the others were always kind as well as critical. I had two main problems, they told me. First, I often sang off-key. I didn't know it—and had to work hard to hear that in myself. Second, and so interesting to me, I *performed* my songs too much. Since I'm an actor, I tended to see them as little monologues, whereas most singers focused on the music itself. I never really gave up my style—I didn't want to—but I worked to connect the music more intimately with the lyrics.

Over the months, this group of women who seemed to have very little in common besides the music grew close in respect and care for one another. For a long time, I was intimidated by the skill and knowledge of the other women and my lack thereof. But their affection for me grew, and that as well as just doing it so much gave me new skill and confidence. Each of us had her own reason for wanting the group, I might say needing it, and we attended religiously. We grew close as friends as well as fellow singers.

From them I learned even more. I had entered a new world of singers and music. It's another universe. Theatre was a return, after all. I already knew how to talk the talk; I knew the process. It's exciting that there's more for me, a lady in her seventies, to be *new* at!

Then, after three years, the group drifted apart. The accompanist got a real job: a good one. The Boulder flood of 2013 left us all in crisis for a long time. Afterward, several of the women went off in different directions: two to try to sing professionally and one to teach her own classes. That left Dorinda and me. I miss the group. Their responses became a very part of the songs that I sang. But I suppose it was inevitable. I didn't especially see our group as a preparation to perform in public, and the others did. In truth, the desire to perform has soured for me of late, and I don't want it—at least, not now. But I flourished because of the response of the women themselves, whom I had come to cherish.

Maybe Dorinda and I can form another group; I don't know. For now, as I continue taking classes with her, the pleasure of bringing a song to life remains. I become a better singer all the time, and I am always finding more songs to claim as mine. This new world really is a piece of the "more life" that I imagined, without having a name for it when I retired.

At the same time, I have discovered that singing is actually a way to bring my past into my present. Now that I know the basics, Dorinda and I have evolved a different kind of lesson. After my warm-up exercises, I sing the song that I have prepared. But then we start to play around with songs that come back to us on the spot, as we are reminded of other shows and singers. "Do you remember?" we say. She has a life full of lyrics in her head, but so do I. I remember everything: songs from shows of the 1940s, 1950s, 1960s—*The King and I* or *Kiss Me Kate*, all the singers from Ella and Judy to Gram Parsons, Emmy Lou Harris, Linda Ronstadt, and anything by Cole Porter. One lesson led us to The Roches. Another to The Weavers and, out of nowhere, Harry Belafonte! We sing a little of this and a little of that, and when I find a song that sticks, I work on it to make it mine.

In this way, my past comes alive in a literal way: I am singing it. The words and tunes have been in me for so long, and when they emerge now, as I stand in front of Dorinda's piano, with the wrinkles on my face, the pain in my knee, and the knowledge that I mustn't sway my hips too much, I am singing with a present consciousness that literally crosses with a former consciousness. I am ten on the living room rug in Providence and seventy-three in a music studio in Boulder: a girl alive with expectation and ambition and an oldish woman with many memories and insecurities about the present. The music lets me inhabit my different selves simultaneously. Here and in other places, I begin to notice times when my present self and former self are not cut off from one another, as I originally believed.

PART II

Family

4

Everything Begins with Janet (1916–2001)

Janet Rosenthal Hecht, my mother, looks out from a photo on my wall. I saw this picture in her house when I was visiting her in her old age, and I asked if I might have it. It is the quintessential Janet, on the tennis courts in a little white tennis skirt, not posed but in action, the head of her racket a little blurry. A small, pretty woman with short blond hair and strong legs and arms, she is intent and focused on the game.

This photo was taken some time in the 1950s, when I was growing up. I lived with my family in a small gray frame house on Providence's East Side, a primarily middle-class Jewish area. We were two parents, two children, and one little dog.

"Everything begins with Janet" because *I* begin with Janet, literally and also psychologically. She was my mother; I was her oldest child. My sister, Kathy, is three years younger than I am. I looked more like my mother, and Kathy looked more like my father. Our temperaments also matched up. People always said that I was my mother's child and Kathy was my father's child: Was this true? All I knew was that she was the boss of our family, and she concentrated more on me. This created a connection between us, a web of emotions including love, envy, fear, and anger, which was both powerful and lifelong.

My mother died when she was eighty-three, but her importance to me has never diminished. Lately, now that I am in my seventies, I have begun to think about her aging: trying to look at it from the perspective of my own recent experiences and to see beyond the way that it seemed to me during my forties and fifties in the 1980s and 1990s. When I watched her growing old, I was disappointed and angry, with little compassion for her. When I look at that photograph, I am reminded of what a vital person she was in the world, whatever else she may have been. She was so strong. I believed that when she grew older, she would show me how growing old was done. This did not happen, however, for she never understood that age was anything but something to be ignored and/or overcome, even as she kept her hair as blond as it always was. This only increased my disappointment and anger.

It is my job now, it seems to me, to learn from what she did do. I am only twelve years younger now than she was when she died. I look at my thin, veiny hands, so much like hers, and wonder, "How *are* we connected really? What is our difference? Who was she beyond the stories that I have told about her all of my life? Who am I, if I can step out of my thralldom to those stories?"

Yet to understand how I got here, the daughter of Janet Hecht, I must go back before I can go forward.

My mother was a restless woman who'd been a chemist before she had children, obtaining an MA from the University of Chicago in the 1940s, when this was no mean feat for a woman. She had stopped working when she became a mother, the usual thing to do, and had busied herself for many years as a tennis player and Girl Scout leader. She even started a troop for disabled girls and earned an MA in Special Education after her children left home.

Janet was smart, energetic, controlling, with a fierce temper. My father was gentle, kind, often passive, and submissive in the face of my mother's rages. My sister kept to herself and out of the fray. I would fly to my father's defense when she was berating him. I have little memory of her anger at me. I expect that I have repressed it carefully. But I know that I am to this day terrified of anger directed at me.

As a child I looked up to her; I thought that she was wonderful. She was cute and spunky, always going or coming from somewhere in one of the snazzy English sports cars that she loved. In my memory there she is, in her tennis whites with brief jaunty skirts, holding her racquet in just the right place. In her neat green Girl Scout leader's dress, which fit her perfectly (not a bit like the shapeless uniform that I, as a member of my troop, had to wear). She wore loafers and nylons with it: small tidy feet. A gold anklet. Her bright cap of short blond curls.

Or in high strappy heels and clinking jewelry, all set for an evening of gin drinks and dancing with men. Not with my father, no; she didn't like to dance with him, she said. He had this way of switching into double time, and she couldn't follow him. I think that she preferred to lead, anyway. But all the men liked her, and she had no lack of partners.

I secretly spent hours in my mother's bedroom, when she wasn't home. The sun would be pouring in the front windows of the large bedroom that my parents shared, each with a separate twin bed. I would sit at her desk, picking up the objects there, one after the other, the pens and notepads, pretending to use them. I would read her date book. I would open the desk drawers and explore the photo albums that she kept there. I would open her closet door to inspect her skirts and dresses. As a teenager I began to borrow the pleated skirts and colorful sweaters without asking her. I'm pretty sure that she yelled at me for this.

At last I would arrive at the dresser: long, low, and painted black and white. There was a perfume tray with bottles lined up, some with silver mesh bulbs for spraying fragrance behind the ears. Evening in Paris in an oval blue vial. There were twin photographs in silver frames, one of my sister and one of me, when we were small.

These pictures were studio portraits: black and white, behind glass frames that had butterflies and tiny birds engraved in the corners. My sister was a darling three-year-old in a dotted Swiss dress with capped sleeves and a wide sash. Her dark hair was short and curly; her hands were in her lap. I was five, scratched knees showing beneath a short, checked pinafore. Hair in lanky braids. Freckles and a large mouth that dominated my face, with the big teeth and big grin. I would compare these two girls, and every time I found myself wanting. I was so far from cute. Pretty? Forget it. I was awkward, uncomfortable, and it showed.

Janet's dresser drawers were her secret places. It was dangerous to look, but I took the chance. There was so much to learn. Underwear! Women's panties and bras (hers neatly padded with white foam rubber) and firm tan rubber girdles. Rolled-up stockings that could be attached with garters.

In the back of her jewelry box was a soft chamois bag, fawn-colored, tied with a leather string. It held gifts that boyfriends had given her, she told me: a small ring and a silver pin shaped like an arrow. The pin was from Freddy-the man-she-didn't-marry. (He grew up to be very rich, to her chagrin.) The ring was from Rocky-who-was-killed-in-the-war. She still had his picture in the back of her drawer. He was so handsome, dark, and brooding into the camera. I handled these items with reverence.

In the quiet of her bedroom, with the little dog sleeping, curled in a white ball at the foot of her bed, the sunlight irradiating each magical object, I studied my mother's private life, again and again, but secretly, so she would never discover that I needed to know about it.

There was of course the public mother, whom I knew all too well. Life in our household revolved around the tennis courts, around when my mother or my father had dates to play, or practice, or, in my mother's case, teach. We ate dinner late or early, depending. I myself resolutely did not play tennis. I couldn't bear to try a backhand or a serve in front of my mother's demanding eye and be found wanting. I was no athlete. I was an artist: I could write, draw, act, and dance.

There was as well the nighttime mother, the party mother. Janet's twin sister Anne was a painter, and together they hung out with the arty crowd. They went to parties in studios and came home very late. The women, my mother and her friends, wore high platform heels with straps and dark red lipstick. They posed for photos: pulling up their low-cut dresses to expose a thigh, cocktail glasses in hand. In this crowd, there were eventually a lot of divorces. Various people married various other people, who had originally been married to various other people.

I would hear my parents' voices late at night after one of the parties. I couldn't sleep, after all, could I, if my mother was going to talk in such a loud voice? I never knew what they were talking about; I heard only the sounds that I had come to hate more than anything: my mother screaming at my father, "You louse. You prick. You jerk." What had my father done? Something at the party? But what? I never knew.

She yelled at him lot, her voice hard with scorn and rage, often as my father sat in his chair before dinner, a martini in his hand, reading the paper with the TV on. Or at the dinner table. Her words rolled over him like waves in a storm. He would just sit there, looking sad, his head bowed a little, but he didn't look at her. He never fought back, so I would do it for him.

I stood and faced her, defending him: he didn't mean it, it wasn't his fault, while my mother stood fierce and tense in the kitchen doorway. She'd tell me that it wasn't my business: that my father was an idiot who couldn't do a single thing without getting it wrong. I could eat in the kitchen, if I talked that way.

Her anger was fierce and frightening, but it was only one aspect of these moments. What came through loud and clear as well was her sense of her own power and authority.

Recently I found one diary that has survived from my late childhood. I was thirteen when I wrote this.

January 7, 1955

I had an awful fight with Mommy. I was playing my Pinafore [album], and you know how I've just got to dance when I hear good music like that, so of course I like the living room to myself. So Mommy waltzes in to read. Now why, with all the rooms in the house, did she have to pick that one! So then I couldn't listen to my

record, 'cause I won't make up dances in front of HER!
I called her selfish and then she blew up and said that I
couldn't play Pinafore for a week!

I told Daddy, however, and he said he'd talk to her.
He'd better. She was in the wrong, but in her eyes she
never is!

<u>Horrors, she could never be wrong.</u>

This diary entry is illuminating to me now, because the fact is
that I have few memories of her anger focused directly on me.

The diary is revealing in another way, as well. In my childhood, my mother championed my theatrical and literary ambitions. The diary shows how the living room dancing was meant
to be private, just for me and not a public performance. I liked
to perform, but it was kind of exhausting, too. I had a private self
that needed to be protected. Mostly, however, I found my private
self in books, for I was and am a voracious reader. Curled up in
the blue upholstered chair in the living room (a more sheltered
space, because it wasn't the "family room"), nibbling on crack-
ers, I would adventure without having to prove myself. The people whom I met in books and the lives that they lived were real
to me, and they kept on reverberating in my head all through
the day. In this way, I had a whole world that was separate from
my life anywhere else. It was private, and it was safe. "Safe" was
important, because the outside world was actually dangerous as
well as rewarding. The other side of success is failure, and neither my mother nor I could accept my not winning the prize, not
getting the part.

My mother loved being a theatre mom, and she was proud
of me for having written a poem chosen for a national children's anthology and for getting straight As in school. For me,

anything that wasn't winning, a B grade, for example, was failure to her. For my part, I needed her praise. It meant that she loved me; this is what I understood. Her criticism or anger meant that she did not. And I so desperately wanted her to love me.

My mother gave love in the form of praise, not affection. My cousin Judy, who was my best friend when we were girls, told me once when we were adults that she did not remember my mother ever hugging me. Weakness of any sort was seen as failure and frowned upon in our family. Illness was a form of weakness, and nobody was supposed to give in to it. She didn't. Yearning for simple displays of affection, as I still do, I always cherished those moments when I was actually sick enough to go to bed, and she would bring me pudding on a bed tray.

Thus I was deeply dependent on her for my sense of identity itself. But praise and validation from her were not a consistent matter. It was conditional, depending on her judgment, even her mood. When did things change between us so that I did not have to try so hard? I think that this happened gradually, beginning when geographical distance itself altered our continuous interactions and gave me some degree of autonomy. As soon as I went to college, I was less under her sway. On her side, when I went to graduate school in my twenties and did not go off to Broadway, which was the plan, she began to have no real interest in what I was doing. (Later, when I became the author of scholarly books, she didn't read them, but she asked me for their book jackets to show to her friends. She still needed a way to show me off.) Perhaps my scholarship came too close to her own past as a scientist, for I was meant to succeed primarily as an artist, I learned. Until she died, she would walk around with the manuscript of my unpublished book of poems, as if they represented the daughter whom she wanted and loved.

But when my devotion to her lessened, the anger that was probably there, too, revealed itself. For example, when I began to have children, she lectured me for continuing my career. For her, a woman with kids and still working at a job was a no-no. She'd known better than to do that. Times had changed, I understood, especially for feminists. But she did not understand and saw my behavior as a challenge to her; this made her very angry. But her belief that this essential part of my life had anything to do with her made *me* angry, too.

When you are a child, you don't analyze your situation. My big aha moment came as an adult in the 1980s when I read Nancy Chodorow's *The Reproduction of Mothering.* There I read a psychoanalytic discussion of the mother-daughter relationship that reverberated painfully with me. Chodorow's work led me to other psychoanalysts, both before and after her, who wrote about the earliest relationship between mothers and babies. I learned about the importance of the mother's recognition of the child's "separate subjectivity." ("Oh, it's you!" says the mother, as she gazes into the eyes of her infant.)

I discovered how things can go awry if this does not happen, particularly if the mother sees the baby as an extension of herself and withdraws her attention when the child does not behave as desired. D. W. Winnicott wrote of how the child then needs to woo the mother for a love that is never unconditional, how this gives that child a strange sense of self-identity. Who is she when the mother averts her gaze?

At last I had explanations, especially in the studies that focused on mothers and daughters. Now I knew something about why I felt and behaved as I did. I struggled in therapy to change these patterns, but it proved difficult, since they went so deep. I remember one of my daughters saying to me when I was in my fifties, as I was anguishing over a moment of her anger that meant to me the loss of her love, "Mom, I am not your mother. Get over it!" Smart girl.

I have told my version of the story of my mother and me over and over in poems and short stories. I have as well focused much of my academic research and writing on the daughter-mother, mother-daughter relationship. Both my feminist and academic training have given me the belief that understanding it and telling it would free me from what Jessica Benjamin called "the bonds of love." Her phrase is a deliberate pun: those bonds are at once a form of intimacy and a form of imprisonment.

But all of this knowledge never did break those bonds. Perhaps this was at least partially because in my relationship with my mother I was alone in the desire to confront our "issues." She didn't think that there were any issues and certainly had no desire to discuss them.

But I also think that I needed my version of the story to help explain important aspects about me as an adult, such as my life-long search for true love; my endless expectation of rejection (me, a woman who has had three very long-term romantic and sexual relationships); my many successes coupled with a deep-seated sense of inadequacy. I believe that all of these feelings and motivations were influenced by my relationship with Janet Hecht.

When my grandmother Sallye died, I asked my mother to send me a necklace that I'd once given to my grandmother. In response, my mother literally bartered the necklace for my poems—poems that I'd deliberately not sent to her. For these were the feminist '70s, so in my writing, I was "telling it like it is," or was. Reluctantly, I sent her the poem collection, where-upon she called to tell me that in the one about the fighting in our family during my childhood I'd gotten it all wrong: "It was never like that," she said.

She still possessed great power over me. My defenses, at-tempts to protect myself, grew strong, but they always warred with my lifelong guilt–maybe it was all my fault, somehow"— and yes, my secret desire for her to be the mother whom I still desired: not a woman who talked about herself only when we were on the phone but one who would let me tell her about my feelings or even tell her about my children. And if I tried to do so, one who would not say that she had to go: she would be late for something or someone was picking her up, even when she was the one who had called me. I called her, too: of course I did. A daughter is supposed to call her mother. But our con-versations always followed the same format. When we hung up, I always wept.

My defenses were strong enough to keep me from visiting too often, but visit I did. A daughter is supposed to visit her mother, and she always said how much she wanted me to come. She had a fantasy of all the good times we had together. She forgot the long silences; she didn't know how deeply her criticism of me or her monologues about herself hurt. I always tried not to show it, however, for I could never bear her anger.

When I was a woman in my fifties, well ensconced in the bit-terness, anger, and perpetual feelings of rejection that that she evoked in me, my mother showed me a pink department store box in which she had carefully saved mementos of me. There I discovered a series of handmade greeting cards that I had giv-en to her when I was about ten. All had drawings and poems, and many were little booklets. In them I had created her as a beautiful, sexy woman—with a temper, yes—adored by men and her family. There is one drawing where she stands in the center of the family, wielding a baseball bat: my father on crutches, my arm in a sling, my sister's head bandaged, and the dog barking. We're all begging her to stop. The caption goes, "Though I've really got to add, her temper's rather bad." The drawing is cute, and it's clearly meant to be funny. But most of the cards are versions of the sexy mom theme.

In some drawings, I literally appear as a lovesick swain. "I've got the no-Mommy blues," sighs a sad figure in blazer and Bermuda shorts, sitting at a table, a bottle and a drink beside her, with a cigarette and smoke rings over her head, while the dog howls. This is a first page of a get-well card, for Mommy is in the hospital with her arm in a cast. In another, she is a showgirl with a pink heart on her bottom (actually a little Valentine's Day candy), and the poem says, "Hollywood will be calling you, with the figure you've got pal, but won't you please, stay at home and be <u>My</u> glamour gal!"

I was amazed. I could not remember loving her like that. I asked to borrow a few of them. She agreed reluctantly but made me promise to send them back. I did, but not before I'd made copies. When she died, I found the box and took it home with me. These cards are the subject of the opening chapter in my last book, which is about the mother-daughter relationship in writing. I printed reproductions of them there, for they show how my own writing and drawing talents gave me yet another venue for trying to win her love, and they are shockingly blatant about it. I who fled from her for most of my adult life.

As I look at the prominent veins on my hands and watch myself grow thinner, I think of my mother as she aged. She dieted throughout her life (her grandmother, I was told, was obese). But when she was in her seventies, she was so thin that my friend Jim called her "a cricket." Mean, funny, and accurate. Yet still she was cute and, with chemical help, still blond. She remained athletic, teaching tennis almost till the end and playing in national senior tournaments. She dressed like a young woman in shorts, T-shirts, and brightly colored pants; she acted like one, too. The wisdom that I imagined she would access was never part of her idea for herself. Jaunty and sexy to the end was her idea.

Yes, sexy. The woman who told me after I returned from my honeymoon at twenty-one, unhappy about my first experiences of intercourse, that she "always had to be on top for anything to happen" had always boldly flaunted her sexuality. This in the 1950s, when it was anything but the traditional public persona for middle-class women. I am thinking now about this sexuality that was so much a part of her persona.

My father divorced my mother in the late 1960s, when he was sixty and she was fifty-six. He left her for a "younger woman" (the lady in question was forty). At long last, to my way of thinking. I never understood why they were married, really, and I actually envied my cousin Judy, whose parents divorced in the 1950s, when such an act was scandalous. Judy had taken me aside and whispered to me this secret, this unspeakable news. Shocked though I was, I remember wishing that this might happen for me, too.

But when my father left home, my mother moaned and wailed about being alone, abandoned. She tried to get him to come back and said he was the love of her life. But he married his girlfriend. Then the newlyweds had a child, which surprised them both.

I learned many years later, from both my mother and my father, that he'd been having affairs for years. My father was a very handsome man, whose friends called him "Greg," after Gregory Peck. When my mother spoke to me about this for the first time, she called the women his "pillows," because they let him tell them his troubles. She didn't think (or care) that he had any troubles. She thought that he was lucky to have her. For his part, my father revealed to me one night over a restaurant dinner with much wine that he'd never wanted to marry her, but that she wanted him. Besides, she was rich, and he was poor.

My mother also told me, these many years later, about the secret affair she'd been having for years. I had no idea about my parents' extramarital sex lives when they divorced and certainly not when I was growing up.

I did know that several years after her divorce she had a public affair with her handyman, Charlie, a married Catholic and a very sweet person. He actually kept clothes in her home. She dated him openly, and they even travelled together. They were an odd couple, but she seemed happy with the arrangement, although she constantly berated him in front of everyone, even as she had done my father before him; they were both stupid, she said. It was embarrassing, but it didn't make me angry the way her treatment of my father had always done. But then, he wasn't my father. This story has a poignant ending. Some years into their relationship, she somehow discovered that Charlie had another lover, too: another woman in whose house he also kept his clothes! The two women actually met and confronted Charlie with his "betrayal": not of his wife, no, but of each other.

Yet my mother was devastated for a long while, for she had actually loved him, I suppose.

Later, when she was in her seventies, she met a man from California who courted her and with whom she sometimes had sex, she said, but she didn't like him very much. No, she told me wistfully, fingering the gold choker that she always wore around her neck, she had always loved Jerry, with whom she'd had an affair ever since he and his wife lived in Providence and were members of the same crowd back in the 1950s. They'd moved away to Florida, but she'd been having trysts with him ever since: in Florida, when she visited a woman friend; when he came on business to Providence; and even sometimes in other cities, for he was a salesman. *He* was her true love, she declared, but he wouldn't leave his wife for her.

I kept saying "Oh" to all of this and trying to change the subject. I didn't want this information, but she was determined to tell me. I think that these conversations were inappropriate, but now I see as well that she was an unusual woman to be so outspoken about such matters. Didn't we fight for just that right in the feminist 1970s? But I also wonder about her aggressiveness in these matters, although I know that her twin sister was equally overt. I wonder where that came from. Her mother, my grandmother Sallye, was certainly a proper lady, who was shocked by my breastfeeding one of my babies at the dinner table.

But mostly, I felt diminished by her overt sexuality, for I never saw myself as that sort of girl or woman: me, the virgin who'd waited five years from falling in love with her first real boyfriend to graduating from college and marrying him before she'd have sex.

But now I also see her frustration, or worse, in an unhappy marriage with a man whom she did not particularly like—a man who was, she believed, her intellectual and social inferior. No matter how attractive she was, she did not have another marriage after her divorce, making do with such odd and essentially unavailable partners. Most of all, I suddenly see her endless search for romance and love, for surely that's what she meant when she kept saying that this man and that man was her "true love." Maybe a lot of that sexiness was sheer bravado.

Janet persisted at her image of herself well into her sixties and seventies. She continued to diet, dye her hair, and drive her little sports cars; her tireless energy kept her on the courts. True, she had arthritis in her hands and what was then called a "tennis elbow," but these problems seemed more like occasions for complaining than anything that kept her down. Her bout with melanoma came in her sixties. (No wonder, since not only had she spent all those years on the tennis courts, but she'd been tanning herself on the beach and in the backyard all of her life.) But she recovered, and it didn't return. As soon as she left the hospital, she bought herself another new car.

Also, her self-centeredness became even more blatant: she was more demanding and mean-spirited. When my daughter Alex graduated from college in 1986, my mother was in her sixties. I remember that she grouched throughout the weekend: about the rain, about our (admittedly uncomfortable) accommodations in a rather Spartan dormitory, and about our walking too fast to get to an event. But complaining was her style. I was really angry this time, for this was not *her* event, it was my daughter's, and I vowed not to speak to her ever again. I didn't, not for several months—until the debacle with Charlie was revealed, and she called me in tears.

That was Janet when she was aging. Now, as arthritis courses through my body, and I find myself carefully negotiating physical situations so that I won't hurt myself, or just to avoid pain when I can, I think about her behavior at that graduation. I don't *whine* as she did, I hope. But at first I did announce my pain and why I was behaving "out of character," and this bothered my daughters mightily. (I have come to understand that this is a common response by daughters to aging mothers, but it's taken me a long time to learn this, and I still know it intellectually more than emotionally.) Then I simply didn't understand, but for the sake of avoiding their displeasure, I began trying to pretend that that I was just fine in these situations. But I was angry, even as they were at me. I hope (and believe) that my relationship with my daughters is different in profound ways from what I knew with my own mother. But still, just as I wish for their care or sympathy, I remember how I could not give it to her.

At Alex's graduation, I never for a moment thought that Janet might really have something about which to complain. When she always wanted to talk about her medical issues, I never understood that more and more these matters occupy an aging person's life. And most important, I never understood that a daughter might feel anger rather than compassion for a mother who was slipping from her life of many activities and many companions. My mother *wasn't* as strong as she pretended to be. She probably was hurting, even though it was displayed as aggression.

No, we're not the same, even though my greatest fear as I became a woman was that I would turn into her. When I found myself raising my voice at my children, or criticizing my husband, I shuddered inside. I didn't want to be anything like her. But to see that we do share some things at this time in life doesn't make me her, I do understand—although I confess to worrying about it even now. Rather, it gives me a way to look inside her, if only a little.

Then came the time when Janet Rosenthal Hecht was not aging but old. We knew it because she finally stopped dying her hair. The natural gray looked fine, actually, and not so different from the blond. We knew it because her twin sister Anne had died of cancer. My mother was truly alone then.

It is hard to imagine what it must have been like for her without her other self. How she must have wandered through the corridors of her mind, looking for the presence that had been there from the beginning. Oh, they fought like the devil. They were so critical of one another. My mother always said to me, when I would look at myself in mirrors—even the toaster on the kitchen table—that I had better watch out or I would grow up to be vain like my aunt! Yet they were completely dependent upon one another. Once my parents moved to Chicago for his job, a few years after I'd left home, but my mother lasted there about three years before returning to Providence. She needed to come home to her sister. Janet and Anne looked so much alike that once when I was a child, playing with my cousin Judy at her house, a woman came in, and I thought she was my mother. She was my aunt. They proudly told the story of pretending to be the other person to fool boyfriends when they were young. The twins. The twins. How much of my mother was my mother because she was one of the twins?

When Anne died, Janet became profoundly depressed. When I insisted that she see a therapist, she finally went—but stopped after three sessions. "She didn't tell me what to do to fix it," my mother said angrily. "Nothing's changed." When Anne died, my mother grew old.

Then the emphysema came. At first they thought it was asthma. On one of my visits, my mother was really out to please. She took me on a senior outing, traveling by bus to nearby Concord to visit Louisa May Alcott's home (I did not want to see the home of one of my favorite writers turned into a tourist attraction), and then a stop at a make-believe Colonial town, replete with gift shop. The "town" was built on a hill, and my mother said that she didn't want to climb up that street. She sat down on a bench, and I had to see the sights alone. I didn't want to be there at all, so I zipped through the buildings as quickly as I could. I was angry at her, though I never said so, for bringing me there in the first place: for not viewing the stupid buildings with me when she'd made me come. I had no pity, no tolerance.

But ultimately her problem was understood to be emphysema: she had an air tank with a hose and plastic tubes in her nose. She was always afraid that the deliveries would be late, and she would run out. She couldn't breathe in the night and called 911 over and over. "Tough it out," I thought. "That's what you always do." But soon she couldn't climb the steps to her pretty condo by the bay, so she moved into the fanciest assisted living establishment in the area. But she wouldn't make friends there.

"There's no one here like me," she said.

"Well, of course not," I thought. "They're all rich WASPs." She sat in her apartment and complained. It got so the aids wouldn't come because she called them so often, or this is what I inferred from her harping on their unreliability and rudeness.

After a couple of years, she had to leave this place, because she couldn't really afford it. She moved to one that was smaller, less expensive. Then her new apartment was too little, she said. She was bored, she said, as she sat in front of her trusty TV. I replied, "But don't they have groups here that you could join?"

"They're silly," she replied. "I don't want to do those kinds of things."

"Why don't you start your own?" I asked. "Like maybe a reading group. You'd be good at that. You're a good leader." This woman had started the first Girl Scout troop for "handicapped" kids in the state.

"I don't want to," she said. "These people are all stupid. I wouldn't want to talk about books with them. And anyway, I don't read much anymore." And she changed the channel.

Why wouldn't she help herself? That place wasn't so bad. I ate lunch in the pretty dining room, where people sat at tables and chatted. Some stopped by our table, and she proudly introduced me. But then she hissed nasty things about each of them to me.

I didn't get it at all. Now I know that she didn't want or even understand what this life of diminishment had to offer. She didn't know herself there. She couldn't tolerate such a loss.

But I thought, "Why don't you fight? You always fight." That's who she was to me. (That's who I am to my daughters…) Would she have liked me to sympathize? To say, "How awful for you?" Probably. But I wouldn't do that for her.

Old is the story of her frustration and fear, when weakness and disease replaced her trusty strength. I didn't live in her city, and my sister did. Because I wasn't there all the time, I became her fantasy of the good daughter, my sister the bad. She snarled at my sister constantly. But Kathy did the work—without love or grace, but she did it. And I did not. I was not a good daughter. I didn't want responsibility for her and didn't have to take it. When she talked about coming to live with me, I said no, that she couldn't live at this altitude, which had truth in it, I suppose. My sister wouldn't have her at her house, that was for sure.

I felt guilt then, but it didn't stop me from doing what I did— or didn't do. My desire to keep away from her was much, much stronger. Now I feel sorrow for not being able to try to overcome my legacy of pain and anger. Would it have been so bad if I had done more? I think that she would have experienced some kindness when she needed it, even if she didn't exactly know how to let someone be kind to her.

She was dying, but I didn't know. She'd go to the hospital, then a nursing home, and then come home, again, until home wasn't home anymore. That happened so often that it grew to be a pattern. I knew that she could never recover from her disease, but I thought that she'd live a long time with it. Why not? After all, the melanoma didn't kill her. Her own mother had died at ninety-three. I let my sister call the shots, and I went about my life. In April 2001, my sister called and said it was happening again, that it was bad. But she also said not to come. "Maybe I should go this time," I thought. I didn't know what to do, but finally I went.

Janet was in the hospital bed, a small, shrunken person. She was simply bones, and her face looked like a skeleton head. Nevertheless, she was still herself: bitching at the nurses and complaining about the hospital, the food, the pillows. But as I sat beside her, she started to cry. She told me that she wanted to die, but she was clearly struggling to live. This time she frightened me. She *was* dying: I saw it then. Suddenly something inside me turned over: my heart, I guess. I did something that I never remember doing, ever: I held her tiny body and said, "I love you, Mom." It wasn't just to make her feel better. I meant it. She said she knew. And I left the room.

That was it. I went home the next day. Two nights afterward, my sister called to say that she had decided to stop the medications this time, and so my mother had died. My mother, who had taken up so much space in my life for so long, was gone. Still, even at this point, I was shocked. She always bounced back; she would live forever. Dead? I couldn't understand it. Inside me was a hole, and I didn't know what feelings could fill it. I couldn't think what to do. At last I took a white square candle that she had once given me but I had never used and lit it. I sat and stared at it. Then I went to bed.

Janet was cremated at her request. We held a small funeral two weeks later in the chapel of a neighborhood cemetery. As eldest daughter, I spoke, having written all of my words out carefully beforehand, and I said things that I meant but were positive and often humorous. A few others spoke, too. Then my mother was formally dead.

I did not mourn her. Primarily what I felt was relief. It was a freedom that I had never known before. My long struggle with her was no longer like a sword hanging over my head, always poised for another opportunity to strike. However, her enduring power lives on in my own existence. I am her daughter, and all that I have been and still am is informed by the power of that relationship. I have wanted her. I have run from her. I have hated her. I have loved her.

But I never let myself know her. What would that have been like? Impossible then. My own responses to her as a child forced me to create a fantasy person, an idealized (both good and bad) icon: a capital "M" mother instead of a mother. But my Mother is dead, and the battle has ceased.

To start to know her, if only a little, is all that I can manage, but my aging hovering over her aging helps me. I do see some of her weakness and struggles so that suddenly she seems less than all-powerful. Primarily I am aware of her frustration, brought to a head during her aging years, when the strength and willpower that carried her through so much was consistently weakening.

If I look back, I can see how it must have been present in many areas of her life—her unhappy marriage and disappointing affairs. (Why *did* she choose men who were not her equal in any way?) I have thought a great deal about her intelligence, which I inherited from her. She was the twin who went to graduate school and who was a chemist. Did that mean nothing later? She became a helper and teacher: of tennis, in Girl Scouts, and later in Special Education. From all accounts—hers and her students'—she was very good at this and found it gratifying. But when she went back to school to earn that MA in special education after my sister and I grew up, she told me, "What I really want to study is psychology, but I'm too old." She had all that energy and kept so busy, but still. An interesting fact about her tennis playing is that she did not like to compete, she said, and did so only as a much older woman, when she knew that she would be better than most of the other people with whom she was playing.

Her twin Anne was so much happier than my mother. She had a second husband whom she loved, and she worked as a painter, at which she was very successful. She, too, had that temper, but if you study photos of the two women, who look almost exactly the same, you see that my mother's face is so much tenser. How did Anne's happiness make my mother feel?

I know very little about her relationships with her parents, except that she identified with her father. "He was the smart one." But he was not, apparently, a very good stockbroker, and he lost a great deal of money in 1929. The twins were raised with wealth and prestige—private schools and maids—and much of that was gone after the crash. She surely must have been deeply bitter about that. Although my father was her choice, he never could provide the kind of life from which she had come.

I think about her behavior at Alex's graduation, when no one expected that she might find the circumstances difficult, or in the assisted-living homes when she kept to her tiny apartment and would not join in, and I see how sad it all was. Emphysema, a debilitating disease, took her from her tennis and her home. It left her powerless, as it slowly killed her. Her sister died, and her two daughters did not care about her.

I had no pity, even as I had no understanding. I am guilty of that, and I am sorry. But still, even with this new sense of her, I do not mourn her. I was afraid of her, always—afraid of the emotional damage that she could always cause me. Did she know that she was doing it? I really don't think so. But still I can't forgive, although I am told that is the healthy thing to do. Even though I now see the outlines of a person and not only a queen or a gorgon, my life is my life because she was my mother. Her gifts and her punishments are entangled around my heart.

5

Philip J. Hecht, My Father (1913–2003)

I have spoken at length about my relationship with my mother. It dominated my childhood and remained a powerful presence as long as she lived. Even now, when I am in my seventies and she has been dead for over ten years, she looms in my consciousness. I am her daughter, whoever else I may be. But I had a father as well, Philip Julius Hecht. He served as a counterpart to her in their marriage, for they were very different from one another; in the same way, my relationship with him was very different from what I experienced with her. I trusted him completely and saw him as a steady source of quiet love. Only now do I understand how much more complicated our relationship actually was.

In his mideighties, my father visited me in Boulder for the first time in twenty years. I think that as he grew old, he finally decided that our long separation should be overcome. Especially, he wanted to know his grandchildren, whom he had never met. It was his second wife who had decreed this separation. "Stay away from your first family," she'd said, and he had more or less obeyed.

When he appeared, he was handsome and charming as always, with his warm brown eyes and aquiline nose (the family thought of it as a "Jewish nose"). His once-dark wavy hair was now gray and sparser, but his expression was just as sweet. We had lovely dinners together, walked in the foothills and on the pedestrian mall. Suddenly my daughter's kids had a great-grandfather. He tried very hard to enter their world, and they responded to him happily. But there is one photo from our visit to the Butterfly Pavilion, with Phil sitting on a bench between my young granddaughters, Emma and Eliza. They are looking at him, and he is looking off into the distance. He is not present to them at all. This behavior was also characteristic of my father. He could be totally involved and then not. This was an aspect of his personality that I completely disregarded in my childhood and young adulthood.

When I was a child, he was good to me, loving and attentive. He was a mild man, kind and sweet. But he did like to flirt, and his very gentleness enhanced his charm, along with his good looks. Like most people, I found him very attractive, especially when I was a teenager. He would dance with me at parties, and I learned to follow him, even as he moved into double time. He made me feel special.

But when I was an adult in my thirties and he was sixty, he more or less abandoned me. He divorced my mother, remarried, had a child, and then had little to do with me or my sister, except for the occasional phone call. Still, there were the dinner dates we had when I was visiting my mother. Our dinners were indeed like dates, with all the trappings. Drinks, fancy restaurants, confidences: I was proud to be the woman across the table from him. For I continued to adore him, even when he behaved badly or disappointingly to me. It is only now that I see how much I simplified our attachment. I needed my belief in his enduring love. I believed in it long after it was gone. Consequently, in his own way, albeit it was not my mother's way, his love for me was neither simple nor straightforward. It had a dark side—not cruelty but thoughtlessness. He didn't see that using the seductive behavior that worked so well with adults was out of place with a young girl. I believe that it was a way to counter the power of the women he married and that his other strategy, disappearing down a rabbit hole of his own devising for self-protection, was a technique that could hurt more people than the wife whom he wanted to escape. He never intended to hurt *me*. Yet in the end, his behavior became part of my precarious understanding of the love to which I was entitled and the love for which I yearned.

My parents both grew up in Chicago, but whereas my mother came from a wealthy German Jewish family, my father, although also German Jewish, came from the lower middle class. He did not go to college as a young man. In truth, he spoke very little about his early life, and then only much later, when my daughters as adults would question him. Consequently, my information about his childhood and his family is minimal. I met his parents and his brother once, but that was all. He told us that he'd had an uncle who was an opera singer.

My aunt Anne met her husband, Ted Kolb, when she was a student at the Art Institute of Chicago. She moved to Providence after they married. Uncle Ted's family owned the Peerless Company, a department store there, where he became a manager. My mother must have badly wanted to follow her sister, so Ted promised my father a job at the store. That's why my parents moved to Providence. Philip sold ties at Peerless for a while, but later he struck out on this own and became a salesman at a company that anodized aluminum—that is, colored the metal. This was his job when I was a child. He was a businessman, who came home every night to his martini, his paper, and his angry wife.

In his late fifties, however, Philip was forced into early retirement: whereupon he went to college! After graduating from Rhode Island College with a degree in general education, he earned not one but two master's degrees, one in history and one in English, followed by a PhD in history from the University of Rhode Island. He was also interested in psychology and especially the work of psychoanalyst Theodor Reik. By then he was in his seventies. Afterward he taught Western Civilization at several community colleges. He was still teaching when he died. The president of the college where he then taught discovered his age only when he read my father's obituary, or so he said.

I love the story of his later life: how this working-class boy who married a rich girl finally struck out on his own after sixty! Unfortunately, he married a smart, energetic, professional woman who turned out to be a lot like my mother—and kept him under her thumb in his domestic life. This included turning him against his two daughters and their families, because for her there was only one child: their child, his son. His weakness and passivity didn't go away. Nonetheless, in the outside world, he managed to find himself at last. With no help from anyone, he created Phil Hecht anew: a student, a teacher. I didn't know his mother. I can't say why his difficulties with women were his Achilles heel. I knew him only later.

My father was such a nice man, from the days when he willingly donned a tutu and did a silly dance for the parents' talent show at my grammar school or, earlier still, when my sister and I were small, when he got down on his hands and knees and played lion: two giggling girls trying to escape the not-so-scary monster who would grab us and pretend to gobble us up. He taught me to swim in Wellfleet Bay and hiked with my sister and me on nearby Mt. Monadnock.

I did not know about his affairs, of course, but I did know that he was popular with his friends. Group photos from the 1950s show him at the center of "the gang," many of their faces turned toward him with pleasure. I was proud that he was my father.

Another memory of him has stayed with me always, and it is a clue to his other mode, something that I ignored in my general sense of him. In my first semester of college, I was very homesick. When I was home for Christmas, I sought out my father for help. I was probably afraid to tell my mother. We were sitting in his parked car, talking in the rain, which made large wet splashes on the windshield. I cried and told him of my misery, that I did not want to go back. I wanted sympathy for starters and help. He said, "Well, Suzy, we often have to do things that we don't want to do." That was that. When I would come to him, as a teenager and then an adult, to ask for help, his answer was always the same: "Stop fighting things so much. Let things take their course." But all those years, I kept trying for more from him, believing that he could give it to me.

I didn't understand that this passivity was the flip side of his charm: in his marriage and in his life. I don't think that he sought out those women with whom he had affairs; I think that they chose him. They belonged to my parents' group of artistic friends. They all prided themselves on being "Bohemian," and even as there were many changes of partners during their heyday in the 1950s, there must have been sexual adventuring as well.

I imagine that the woman who became his second wife pushed him to get the divorce. She was a psychiatric social worker and in fact a version of my mother, smart and assertive, clearly the stronger partner. We were living in Vermont then, and out of the blue, there came a phone call from Philip, saying that he wanted to fly up from Providence and visit us. He would not say why, only that he would tell us when he came. Fly? I thought that there was something seriously wrong. The first thing that I imagined was cancer: my father? my mother? After his martinis, he told us. Hesitatingly, he said that he wanted to get a divorce.

I was happy for him. I thought that he would live his life at last, free from my mother's control and rages. Unfortunately, he was actually entering another cage, but that night I saw that he wanted something like my permission or maybe my blessing. He was beginning to assert himself at last, but at that point, he probably felt guilty, too. From my point of view, as the daughter of his marriage with my mother, I willingly gave both.

Actually, during my childhood my father did find his soul someplace: not in his job and not even on the tennis courts, a sport that he enjoyed all of his life. For tennis was my mother's terrain. He came alive at the tiller of his sailboat. Out on the water, his passion surfaced.

He'd learned to sail on Lake Michigan, but I knew him as the captain of sailboats on Narragansett Bay in Rhode Island. In the beginning, there was a small craft that he bought with his brother-in-law, the *AnnJan*, named for my mother and her sister. As the years passed, the boats grew bigger and bigger. He raced them with crews and even took jaunts down the eastern seaboard. The enlarged photo that I display among my family pictures shows him at the tiller, squinting into the sun, waves and sky behind him. He looks like a hero, a bold adventurer. Such a contrast to the rest of his life! (And a clue to the man he became much later.)

My mother didn't like the boats. They occupied too much of his time: not just the sailing itself but the preparing of them to go into the water and the taking them out of the water and winterizing them. When she came along to sail, she'd lie out on the front deck and sunbathe, while all the activity took place in the cockpit. I liked the front deck, too, so much closer to the water as we moved swiftly forward. But I learned what to do in the cockpit when the boom came around (move quickly to the other side of the boat and bend to avoid that heavy wooden bar), and sometimes I even was allowed to steer the tiller, usually with his guiding hands beside mine. I, too, loved the deep water: the smell of brine, the roil of the waves, the long stretch of bay that met the horizon. Aboard the boat, sails full as we headed into the wind, I idolized his skill and his command. This was the only place in his life where he became such a person: captain of the ship.

After my marriage, we would visit with my parents at their home for Christmas, for I had not yet broken away. Once they came to our house in Bennington, and we all made dough ornaments, a few of which exist to this day. Little Santas and stars. A few remain, dried and roughened and fragile with time. But then came the divorce, and though my mother visited my house for a few more Christmases, my father was out of the picture.

My father did not know his grandchildren, neither my kids nor my sister's, even though Kathy lived in the same city. When his new wife, Alcee, who was then forty, suddenly had a baby soon after their marriage, a son, that was the end for me and my sister, and for our children, too. Alcee didn't want his earlier thirty-year stint at fatherdom to exist, and so, presto, it didn't. His daughters all but vanished from his life. He would sneak birthday presents to my sister for her children's birthdays, but he wouldn't come into the party, and he never saw her otherwise. For my part, there were those clandestine dinner dates that I had with him when I was occasionally in Providence. He'd pick me up at my mother's house, and the two of them would exchange some semiflirtatious remarks (!). Then he and I would be off to a seaside restaurant. With the lovely smell of salt wafting through the windows, he'd have his customary martini, and I'd have a glass of wine before dinner; then there would be more wine later for both of us.

After his drink and some wine, he even confided in me. I learned about his marriage to my mother: how it was she who wanted *him*. She was so strong—and rich, he said, and she always got what she wanted. What could he do?

His confidences were rare but momentous. During one of his late-life visits to Boulder, before dinner at my house, after he'd had a few drinks, we were having another of our heart-to-heart talks. That was the moment that changed everything for me: he told me that he had always been angry at me for deserting him after he'd married Alcee, because I never got to know his favorite child, his son. What a doozy, from *my desertion* to what was probably worse: his *favorite child*. I don't really remember what I said to that. I have never forgiven it or recovered from it. But right then? I think maybe I went to cook dinner.

Still, I decided to visit him for his ninetieth birthday. It seemed only right and something that I wanted to do. We—Philip, Alcee, and his son Paul—went out to dinner to celebrate, but I gather that they hadn't been planning anything like that until I showed up. They lived in Ithaca then, because Paul was in graduate school at Cornell. Alcee couldn't live without her son, so my father had agreed to leave Providence, where he'd lived for sixty years, and all his tennis pals and his sailing pals, to move to Ithaca in his eighties. And he got himself a job at the community college there.

Surprisingly, it was a good visit. Everyone, even Alcee, was welcoming. It was nice to spend time with my father. I also really liked Paul, in spite of myself. He turned out to be an aspiring English professor with talents close to my own: he wrote poetry and acted. He loved literature, as well. He was sweet and funny and smart, and we had lots to talk about. Too bad that we'd been strangers for thirty years.

That was May 2003. Philip died in early October of that year from a brain tumor that had gone undetected for months. His dying was peaceful; he simply grew weaker and weaker. The doctors had predicted about three months for him to live, said Paul when he called me in late September. But in October, during the very night before I and my daughters were scheduled to arrive, he died.

There was no funeral. There was, later, a party at his yacht club back in Rhode Island, but I was told that I was not invited. Those were his friends; Alcee and Paul were his family.

Having just seen him on his birthday made his death better somehow, but also worse. If I hadn't seen him so recently, he would have remained that shadowy figure, my faraway father. But we'd been together; we'd talked and made morning tea. For three days, I had been a member of his little family. I missed him, and I felt the hurt of being excluded from the memorial event. The latter was probably foolish: I had been excluded for thirty years. But my feelings upon his death brought home how much the whole scenario had always hurt, even as I thought I was used to it. I'd wanted to see him one last time and say good-bye. But I didn't, and I was left high and dry.

High and dry: but wasn't I always? He was a tangential presence in my life and had been so for a very long time. Present for some purposes, not present for others. He'd had, as they say, a good life, especially in his last years, when he started over and realized many of his dreams. I just wasn't a part of them. I was deeply shaken for some time, because of the fact of death itself and because I loved him. But the feelings have grown quieter.

Here is one more story about Philip, an epilogue of sorts. One night when I was visiting in Providence, he told me that he had cashed in an insurance policy and was giving me and my sister $50,000 apiece. "How kind," I thought. But why then? He was not that old. He told me the reason: his wife had insisted that he leave us nothing in his will. His entire estate, such as it was, would go to his son alone. And he did want to give us something.

After he died, I had to sign legal papers relinquishing my right to anything in his estate. He had very little money. That part hardly mattered. But the rest? I walked across campus to the office of a notary public with a darkness spreading in my heart. I think that those words—"my favorite child, my son"—had finally found their home. When I signed that document, I knew that he had in effect wiped out our life together. Maybe he didn't "want" to do it. But what does that mean? In the end, he was responsible for his actions, no matter whose orders he was obeying. And responsible for his words. How could I forgive that?

These were my parents. I always contrasted my father's delight in me (when we were together) to my mother's coldness and my delight in him (when we were together) to my anger at her. I understood neither that he, too, had been culpable nor that she, too, had been an object of my desire. Together, however, they helped to determine who I have become and to form the source of my emotional life. In truth, they were both objects of desire for me, and both were inconsistent in the love that they offered.

When I consider the experiences of strong but often thwarted desire and the fear of rejection and of anger that have plagued me for much of my life and still do, I need to understand the source. Writing of my first loves from my present vantage point helps me to see not only what these relationships were like when I was very young but also how the patterns that they created live in me still, even as my dead parents live forever in my psyche.

Postscript. Grandma Sallye: Selma Rosenthal (1882–1976)

I am a granddaughter as well as a grandmother. I met my father's mother only once, and I don't remember her. She died when I was a child. But my mother's mother, Grandma Sallye, Selma Rosenthal, was a part of my life. She lived in Chicago, but she made regular visits to us. She slept in my room, and I had to sleep on a foldout cot in my sister's room. We did *not* like sharing, but it was just for a week. Years later, however, when she was in her eighties, Grandma Sallye moved to Providence and lived near us in what was called a residential hotel. I was in college by then, but still, at last she was no longer a long-distance grandmother.

Grandma Sallye matters: when I was a child I adored her. I didn't see her very often, it's true. But my memories of her are special, and they add to my sense of my heritage in a way that was different from what I was given by my parents.

Selma Rosenthal was a stout Jewish matron, who had been wealthy until my grandfather lost a great deal of money in the crash of '29 but who remained, as they say, well off. I was told that she wanted to be a pianist but that "naturally" she gave that up when she married. My grandfather died in 1952 when I was ten, so my grandmother, who lived into her nineties, was a widow for a very long time. My mother always said that she loved her father best. Nevertheless, Janet and her twin sister had a special connection with their mother, for they were born on her birthday.

I keep three photos of my grandmother on my bookshelf. The first is very old, small, and opens like a book. One side is brown velvet; the other shows a lovely young woman inside an oval gilt frame. She wears a large hat and a dress with a high collar, her hair is pinned up high, and she looks seriously at the camera. I think that she looks a little like me at that age. The second is a snapshot taken when she was an old woman, sitting quietly with her knitting in her lap, again unsmiling. I have already described the third, taken outside, where she is wearing a dark coat and hat. Here she is plump and middle-aged, as always staring seriously into the camera. Standing beside her, nestled into her shoulder, also unsmiling, scowling, even, is me: a child in a pale dress with bangs and pigtails. These were my mother's photos, originally. Now they are mine.

My other memories of my grandmother are also like snapshots. They are few but clear. A gold ring with a silver *S* on the top, engraved inside with the words "from Grandma Pet." A long line of Rockettes kicking. Pudding from the New York City Automat, taken from a revolving dispensary.

I cherished my gold ring and kept it well into my adult years, until one of my kids "borrowed" it—then lost it. I saw the Rockettes when my grandmother took me to New York for the weekend on the train when I was ten. I marveled at the Automat and felt very grand at the Brass Rail restaurant.

After my grandfather died, my grandmother "gave up house-keeping," as she phrased it and moved to a residential hotel in Chicago. My family had dinner there once, served in her apartment by her former maid, who helped her out on special occasions. We ate tenderloin steak: the epitome of luxury. When she grew much older and moved to Providence to be near her daughters, she lived in another such hotel, although much more modest. Sometimes my mother and I lunched with her in their dining room on chicken salad. Grandma Sallye died at ninety-three in the late '70s.

My cousin Judy told me the story of her death. Grandma Sallye had fallen, breaking some fingers. She had to be waited on, and she hated that. And so she decided that it was time to die. She asked her daughters to come to her apartment for a visit. Then she asked them to give her a drink. Scotch, I believe it was. Though she was a lady, that was her favorite alcoholic beverage. But when she was old, she was forbidden to drink whiskey. Her daughters knew that, and they knew as well that she asked for the drink because it could kill her. Nevertheless, they gave it to her, and she died.

This is a family myth, but I didn't hear a word of it from my mother or my aunt. My three cousins, my sister, and I shared it. We used to try to imagine what our mothers were thinking. Did they want to please her? Did they hate her? They murdered their mother: that is all we know.

Some of my own memories of my grandmother are critical of her. She used to sit and knit on the sofa, and when she did so, she clicked her false teeth. I would sit across the room, waiting for the next click and grimacing each time. She was always knitting, that woman. She taught me how to knit, too, when I was a child. I loved her for that, and the lessons were part of our special time together. But then the knitting turned on me and made me furious.

As did that time when I came to the dinner table with my first child and tried to breastfeed the baby under a little blanket, and she told me that I was disgusting and made me leave the room.

Once I brought Joseph to visit her in her hotel apartment, and she said nastily that his hair was "all at sixes and at sevens." It was, actually, but that wasn't a very nice thing to say to my new boyfriend. We laughed when she said it. "What did she know?" we thought with the callowness of youth. But she made me angry, no matter that the event turned into a funny family story.

I think now that these anecdotes are actually more critical of me than of her, for they show my youthful lack of tolerance—and understanding—of an old woman. But I have one more story to tell, and it is truly important in its relevance to her meaning in my life. I believe that my father told it to me, late in his life.

Apparently my parents had lived with my mother's parents during the first year of my life. My father was poor, and they'd been trying to "establish" themselves. My grandmother's room was near mine, and sometimes she used to come pick me up and hold me when I cried in the night. Obviously my mother wouldn't have done that, I know, from all that she said to me when I was a young mother about the dangers of picking up crying babies. And so I think—but I don't know for sure—that there was someone in my life at that crucial time who did hold me, if only sometimes. So perhaps I did have a template for my own habitual impulse to touch and to hold, certainly something that I did with my own children. If that someone was my Grandma's Pet, no wonder I loved her so much.

This is just an idea that I have, but I like it.

Segue: Growing Up

School

My 1959 high-school yearbook photo shows me with my characteristic ponytail, very short bangs, full lips, and freckles. The small smile had been practiced. Usually my smile was wide and showed all of my teeth, and I didn't like that. (I still don't in photographs.) I never wore my thin brown hair down until I went to Bennington College, the "Greenwich Village of the North," where we all wore black turtlenecks and long loose hair. "Get your hair out of your face," my father would say. "I can't even see you." But to me, as to the rest of the Bennington students, unrestrained long hair was a symbol of our lives at Bennington. With its fostering of the independent spirit, Bennington was a great change from Hope High School, and it was exactly what I wanted for myself.

Bennington reinforced what my mother wanted for me, too. "Growing up" in these years didn't mean challenging my mother's vision for me. Unconventional, artistic—that was Suzy in her eyes and in mine. It wasn't until I became a mother and then a budding scholar in graduate school that a rift grew between us. Nonetheless, each school had its own lessons for me. Revisiting those years gives me a valuable sense of how I grew from a girl into a young woman entering her adult life.

Hope High School

In high school the pull of being normal was very strong. I don't remember suffering in that way before. In my junior year, I made my biggest effort to belong to the world of regular girls: I tried to join a high-school sorority. Wendy, an old friend from grammar school, nominated me. I went through many of the pledging rituals. I wore my clothes backward to school; I wore my pajamas to school; I wore bright red lipstick and lots of makeup (not my style) to school. But one day I stepped back and asked myself, "Why are you doing this, anyway? You are making a fool of yourself so you can have meetings with these girls? But when you do"—I faced what I knew to be the truth—"they won't like you, anyway." So I stopped. I didn't tell anyone. I just stopped doing the tasks, stopped going to the meetings where they would tell you what to do next. And no one said anything. Then I knew how futile the gesture had been all along.

Because in fact really I was arty, and I dressed the part. I never wore circle pins, button-down shirts, straight skirts, or saddle shoes. I wore black tights and Capezio flats that looked like ballet slippers, with full or maybe pleated skirts. I never had a pageboy haircut. My hair was long, worn in that ponytail. Plus I was smart: I was a straight-A student, except for one B, which I hadn't actually earned. Miss Ethier, the history teacher, gave it to me. When I challenged her, she said it was because I waved my ponytail around too much.

I liked classes, even history with mean Miss Ethier. It's true, though, even after I had proved that I could get an A in physics

(I never understood it, but I was good at studying), I switched the next semester to art classes. I stayed with art, too, when I had the choice between it and typing. I didn't see why I would need *that*, when actually it was one of the biggest mistakes of my life. Many papers and books later, I still type with three fingers!

I was odd in other ways. They said that I was too dramatic and too emotional, something that I had been told all of my life. My camp friends had once said in a session of "truth-telling" that I waved my arms around too much. These may be signs of why I wanted to act, but it didn't help my social life. (Maybe other girls were emotional inside, but they didn't show it.)

But despite the clothing, I was very unhappy with myself. I wasn't pretty (my mother definitely concurred), with those big lips and big nose. I didn't count my large eyes that changed colors from blue to green to gray, depending on what I was wearing. Not being pretty had begun to matter a lot in high school, for I was in my teens, old enough to consider boys and the matter of romance.

I suffered intense unreciprocated crushes on a few of them, and I was once fixed up with someone whom I dated for a very short while. But mostly, I didn't know any boys at my school like me, so mostly boys didn't notice me. "Maybe someday older boys will appreciate you" was my mother's mantra. How would she know, I thought, when she had been dating from her early teens? She was right on this one, though. Later I started dating a couple of young men from my theatre world. Then, when I was fifteen, I met Joseph, who was nineteen, a freshman at Brown University, who'd come to our high school to start a debating society. We fell in love, and that was that. He was my true love, and I was his. My romantic life was settled.

Hope High was a big public school, and that meant that the students came from all levels of social class and many religious, ethnic, and racial groups, especially Portuguese and "Negro," along with Caucasian. This wasn't an issue for me, though, even back in the 1950s: I expect because for the most part we carefully self-segregated one another.

However, I see now that my group of friends were an exception to this social rule. Sandy's family was of Portuguese descent, and her family was poor, but she was really smart, and that was why we gravitated to one another. My best friend was a very religious Christian, who ultimately went to a missionary college, the approved choice for her faith. Her family was also poor. Carol was a Quaker, whose father designed fine china, but they were far from wealthy. There was as well a second group of friends who did not belong to the first: we were Jewish. Sheila was an Orthodox Jew, whose father was a rabbi; Margie was a Conservative Jew with a businessman father. All of us were excellent students: that was the bottom line. But it's telling that there was a gap between the Jewish girls and the others. Except for Margie and Sheila, I would not have known the rest, except that our intelligence set us apart from other students and brought us together. Having these friends was a wonderful experience, really, but I didn't know that then.

My school provided the experience of something one might call the "real world," and I learned there how much high intelligence was disliked by "regular" kids. It was in fact a preparation, not for college, not for my profession, but for much of what I have experienced since retirement. Trying to fit in with nonuniversity people here in Boulder, who by and large do not like the university at all, I have needed to censor my remarks again and again.

Bennington College

I was so glad to go to college. I thought that my real life would begin there. I was happy with my choice of a small women's college that emphasized the arts. I wrote poetry with Howard Nemerov (who became an American Poet Laureate) and fiction with the great Bernard Malamud. The theatre department wasn't as illustrious there as the literature, art, music, and dance departments, but I could take acting classes and act all year in shows. I also studied dance, drawing, sculpture, and printmaking. I was actually a talented artist, and although it was peripheral to me in high school, I won a scholarship to Saturday classes at the Rhode Island School of Design, a prestigious art college.

The academic faculty at Bennington were not as famous as their colleagues in the arts, who could commute to Bennington but still have an active creative life in New York City. But they were good at what they did, and I reveled in the chance to learn subjects that were brand new to me: anthropology and philosophy. Of course, the philosophy that I chose was mysticism, where I studied the Kabala and Taoism: a Bennington kind of class.

Literature courses were equally unconventional. I took one called The Epic, in which we studied two books only: *The Odyssey* on Tuesdays and Joyce's *Ulysses* on Thursdays, page by page. In Epic Romance and Fairy Tale, we read Thomas Mann's *Joseph and His Brothers*, T. H. White's *The Once and Future King*, and J. R. R. Tolkien's *The Lord of the Rings*, using the original hardback British volumes (the book hadn't been published in America yet). With that book I barricaded myself in my room for a weekend, emerging for meals only, and read all three volumes at once. Eclectic? Yes indeed.

The only standard English classes that I took was on British Renaissance poets, with a brand-new PhD named Barbara Herrnstein Smith, who was straight out of graduate school and didn't quite fit into the Bennington mode. She later became a famous literary scholar. But I adored the poetry. I also studied literary criticism with her. I was learning a little bit about how to think about literature in a more conventional manner.

I loved going to a tiny women's college. With its 450 students, Bennington was one more example of that small society to which I am always drawn. Little white wooden dormitories that we called houses lined each side of the "Green," and in them I lived with a close group of friends for four years. In our senior year, I shared a suite with four of these girls. We were two theatre majors, one literature major, and two dance majors, respectively.

Bennington was founded in the 1940s as a liberal arts college for women. It was a progressive institution, with a philosophy that emphasized the development of independent thinking and creativity in each student. Bennington put into practice many of the ideas of the educational philosopher John Dewey, who stressed the need for students to take part in their own learning and promoted the teacher's role as facilitator and guide rather than as font of knowledge. He thought that the ultimate goal of education was to help students possess the full and ready use of all their capacities and use those skills for the greater good.

At Bennington, it was necessary that we develop our own ideas. (I never saw a secondary source while I was there.) Our small classes, often held in the living rooms of our dorms or in the warm weather on the lawn, were a comfortable environment for discussion, with the professor primarily as facilitator. Because it was a women's college—the only men present were the few "dance boys" and "drama boys," there on full scholarship so as to participate in productions—we avoided completely the difficulties that women often face in coeducational settings, such as masculine dominance in the classroom or not wanting to look too smart. We had to establish our own course of study and were encouraged to create independent studies or even new courses, if the material that we wished to study was not in the present curriculum.

We had no grades, only "comments." We had no exams, only papers. I loved creating my own curriculum with the help of my advisor. I worked it out so that I could do not a double major but two full majors: theatre and creative writing. They actually gave me two diplomas! I loved the possibility of making up a course if it wasn't offered. While some students dropped out because of all this freedom, I flourished in it. I actually did invent my own classes as independent studies: most notably, when as a senior I cobbled two courses to apply the literary theory of Kenneth Burke to the poetry of Emily Dickinson, Gerard Manley Hopkins, and Dylan Thomas. The result was a very long essay, of which I was inordinately proud.

Bennington wasn't interested in sending its students to graduate school. Women didn't do that much then. Some students went on to become professional artists of one kind or another, but for the most part, they had their four years to explore their creativity, and that was pretty much that. The college expected them to be mothers with station wagons and three kids. Its goal was that these young women should know how to think and to understand themselves. Our idiosyncratic curriculum, for example, or the time engaged in creative arts, did not prepare me for graduate school. But having learned to be a thinking woman and not be ashamed of it made me in a crucial way more prepared than the other women graduate students with traditional educations, even though when I arrived at Berkeley, I had to take undergraduate courses in Chaucer, Milton, and Shakespeare.

I was also prepared for something else. I came to understand what I was capable of doing on my own and how to think about my self-identity in ways that were not directly influenced by the force of my mother's powerful personality. Even though my achievements as an actor and a poet did not veer from her goals for me, I was ready, although I didn't know it, for conflict with her when the time came. Although never in my life or hers did I move out of the sphere of my profound connection with her, I was ready to have beliefs that were not hers and to fight for them when necessary.

Three days after graduation from Bennington, I married Joseph and became Suzy Juhasz.

6

Motherhood

Alexandra Jeanne Juhasz. Jennifer Anne Juhasz Schwartz. Antonia Janis Juhasz. My daughters. Today my love for them is always with me, always palpable. Yet they are adult women and no longer need an ever-present mother in their full and busy lives. Need is what promotes all that proximity between mother and child for many years. But whereas deep-seated love and everyday affection is important to all of us, at least in my experience it does not lead so readily to ongoing interaction. I miss them. While their adult lives keep them so fully occupied, my side of the equation is not parallel. When you spend so many years responsible for the care and devotion to someone, whatever else you may be doing in your life, those feelings don't just slide away. They have carved too deep a groove in your consciousness. That's why there are so many jokes that poke fun at busybody mothers: "Hi, this is your mother. Call me." Jokes told by adult children. As for me, I still wake every morning and check in mentally on where and how each of my daughters is. I always have; I always will. They are my daughters, and I am their mother.

Motherhood is surely the most complex state that I've ever tried to understand, and as a person (and even as a scholar), I've been attempting to do so for most of my life. Now I am in my seventies, a senior aging woman. This fact has changed my relationships with each one a great deal. Even as I struggled with my mother's aging, so they struggle with mine—and I struggle with their responses to me.

When I look back on my own motherhood, I see how it is intertwined with other essential aspects of my identity and my life: work and feminism. I became a mother before either of these occurred, but I would not be the mother that I am without them. Quite simply, I felt that I needed to work, and I realized this when my first child was a baby, but I do not believe that I could have achieved my work successfully without the advent of second-wave feminism. Then as now, when culture defines motherhood as women's main goal, achievement, and *responsibility*, combining it is an option or a necessity difficulties—and also great gifts, I think—whether it is an option or a necessity. I think that feminism provides a belief structure that women are capable of and entitled to meaningful work *and* rewarding motherhood. (I always remember the nineteenth- and early twentieth-century belief that women were unsuited to higher education because menstruation made them incapable of thinking for days out of every month.) Feminism also has created plans of action to make this more possible.

Therefore, when I tell my story, these factors intertwine over and over in different ways across the years. They are not separate but form the complexity of my own experience as a mother and that of my daughters as my children.

I became a mother before I became an academic: before I got a job, even before I went to graduate school. Eight months and three weeks after I graduated from college, to be precise. What a surprise. I was twenty-two years old and not planning on anything like that. When I got the news, all I could think was "This is not me! I am too young!" Followed by "But I never played with dolls!" I was married immediately after my college graduation, but I never thought about babies.

Forty-plus years ago, I was an innocent. I married my only sweetheart six years after we met when I was still in high school and he was a college freshman. I believed that he was my true love, so that was that. At Bennington College in the early 1960s, the very "Bohemian" students slept with their boyfriends in the dorm rooms, although that was against the rules: rules not about having sex but about having boys in the rooms overnight. When my boyfriend visited, however, he slept in a sleeping bag in the cemetery that was directly outside the campus grounds. He couldn't afford a room in town, and I wouldn't let him sleep in my room. Despite my black turtlenecks, I wouldn't have sex before marriage.

We did "romantic" things together; we just never did "it." I was waiting for the wedding night: Wasn't that the proper way? "It" occurred in Woods Hole, MA, in a small inn; we would take take the ferry in the morning to Nantucket Island for our proper honeymoon. I took off my going-away dress. He asked me to wash my hair, because it was full of hairspray from my wedding hairdo. He wanted me natural. I put on my trousseau nightgown. We went to bed, and I took off my trousseau nightgown. Then sex at last, after years of waiting. Where were the bells and whistles? I didn't feel much of anything. I didn't even bleed. All of my horseback riding at summer camp must have taken care of that. But I was madly in love, and I figured I'd learn how to do it better soon.

Oh, and I had inserted, rather messily and inexpertly, contraceptive foam. The doctor had said that he'd fit me with a diaphragm *after* the honeymoon, since I was a virgin and my size would change. That's what did it—or actually, didn't do it: the foam. It was a lovely honeymoon, at the old Ship's Inn in Nantucket, complete with a widow's walk on the roof. The beach, the dunes, the wild roses, and me in my French bikini—very daring at the time. We couldn't have been happier. True love was real, and it was ours. When we learned three months later that we were to have a child, he was delighted. He was a Catholic.

Joseph was a naval officer then, paying back his navy scholarship to Brown with four years of active service. We were living in a tiny duplex in Norfolk, Virginia, where his ship was stationed. Me? I cleaned the house, read library books, and waited for him to come home at night, when he didn't have overnight duty or the ship was in port. I did *not* write poetry, as I had done all of my life. I simply couldn't. Being alone in the apartment, a wife waiting for a baby, was too much for me. From Bennington straight into this? Sometimes we had dinner with the captain and his wife, for Joseph was executive officer of his ship. I eschewed the Officers' Wives Club. I went once, but I felt so weird, with the centerpieces and ladies in hats and the needlepoint circles. I didn't belong and didn't want to belong. My life to this point had prepared me for none of this. I was going to be an actor. I was going to be a writer. I'd thought that marriage would not interfere with these plans. I was so wrong. My husband was in Norfolk, so I was not in New York. I was a housewife, and I didn't have the wherewithal to write about *that*. And I was pregnant, a girl with a whole new body and a whole new bag of fears.

A week before the due date, I started having contractions. My bag was packed, and that afternoon we drove across the bridge to the Portsmouth Naval Hospital, where a doctor examined me. I remember how surprised he was that I was wearing knee socks. Ah, but I was fresh out of college. He also said that these contractions were not the real thing. "Go home," he said. So back we went across the bridge and lay in our bed, not sleeping. In the middle of the night, I started having contractions again. Were they real?

Weren't they real? They hurt. Finally, they were close enough together to warrant a phone call, and this time we were told, "Come." Back across the bridge once more.

I was put in a cubicle, alone. This was 1964: husbands weren't allowed to stay with their wives in the Portsmouth Naval Hospital. I could hear a woman in another cubicle cursing her husband roundly and saying she'd never let him do that to her again *ever*. So when they asked me what the baby's name would be, I told the nurse that we hadn't decided and could my husband come in and talk to me about it? Of course we'd decided: Alexandra for a girl, Anthony for a boy. But I just wanted to be with him. He came and went again. Then there was only me and the contractions. When we got to the really hard part, they gave me gas. The idea of natural childbirth hadn't reached the Portsmouth Naval Hospital.

Alexandra Jeanne Juhasz was lovely and scary. I held the tiny person in her little receiving blanket and thought, "Oh God,

I am a mother." Joseph was so proud and brought me flowers. In those days new mothers stayed in the hospital for three days, which was just as well, because I had no idea what to do for my beautiful baby. For the first day, she stayed in the nursery, while I recovered from the birth and my milk came in. I was definitely going to nurse her. Many women didn't then, but we had decided that it was right.

Once my breasts were swollen and my milk was there, they wheeled her into my room in her little cot to be fed. I thought that this would be so natural, but she couldn't find my breast and wouldn't stay there when she did. I was afraid to guide her with any firmness, because I thought I would hurt her. She cried; I cried. Then the nurses would give her a little bottle. I didn't want her to have a bottle, but what could I do? The nurses were in charge, and I clearly was not.

On the third night, they left her with me, and we were alone. I was terrified. Finally, when once again I couldn't get her to suck on my breast, I rang the button for the nurse. A large, friendly African American woman came in, and she said kindly, "Try lying down next to her. It will be much easier." Indeed it was. Alexandra curled into me, and my breast was right there where she could find it, where she could hang on tight with her tiny lips, where I could hold her. She began to suck busily, and I cried—happily now. Because we could do it, together, and we were together, we belonged together. She was my baby. And I really was her mother.

My own mother came from Providence once I was home again, because that's what mothers do. Her presence was both good and bad. Good because I needed a mother. Bad because her behavior as my mother was outrageous, and back then I still trusted her. My husband did *not* trust her, not at all, and so I found myself, a very shaky new mother, smack in the middle of a domestic battle. No, Alexandra was smack in the middle, but she and I were in it together now.

Home from the hospital meant no one to ask to find out what to do. Alexandra was a person, a person whom I could hurt. So beautiful, soft, and little. But my mother was there, so I asked her. I asked her everything, but most of the time she couldn't remember. However, she could cook and wash diapers and hang them on the line to dry. And I certainly needed that help.

The war that was fought in that small apartment was over my breastfeeding and the baby's sleep. These were of course connected. For Janet did remember some things: (1) you did not breastfeed babies and (2) babies were to be fed every four hours and put in their cribs. If they woke earlier and cried or didn't go to sleep right away and cried, they were testing you. You did not pick up crying babies.

Joseph thought that these rules were mad. If a baby wanted to be held, pick her up and hold her. I'm not sure where he got these "modern" ideas, but he had them, and I agreed. I didn't want to let my baby cry, when I could hold and cuddle her. But there was my mother, who was furious.

But that wasn't the worst part. My mother thought that the baby cried because she wasn't getting enough to eat! Once Alexandra and I had learned how to do it, that dark hospital night when the wonderful nurse gave her gift to me, my child and I both loved it. These were the happiest moments of our day, so close and warm. That's where the love surged up. Her joy fed mine, and mine fed her along with the warm milk that she sucked. I'm sure that she felt my delight in her, my need for her that perfectly matched her need for me. And now my mother was saying to give her a bottle. I didn't even need Joseph to weigh in here. Wrong, wrong, wrong. I cried, but I refused, and the battle continued until Janet finally went home.

I keep thinking about when my distrust of my mother began, my long anger at her. Because I remember shopping for my trousseau with her during my senior year of college: trying on nightgowns and robes together in a little lingerie shop in Wayland Square. I remember her coming down to Norfolk to help us choose an apartment. Surely then we were mother and daughter, sharing this adventure. I know that I eagerly awaited her arrival when Alexandra was born. I don't think that even her behavior during that visit totally destroyed our relationship, no matter how terrible she was. We got over it. After all, she came again three years later for the second birth: Jenny. But Joseph and I finally decided not to let her come for the third child, Antonia. I think we told her that we were old hands at parenting now. But the truth was that we couldn't bear these visits. I am writing about my motherhood here, but my daughterhood becomes of necessity a part of the tale. Now that I am a grandmother, I know from the other side how true that is.

Alexandra and I spent our first days in the tiny apartment, carrying on our little life together. I had become a housewife in the fullest sense. I cooked and cleaned, but mostly I took care of my baby. I washed her cloth diapers in the machine that my mother had given me for her birth and hung them on the line behind the house. I folded them every evening. I fed her with my milk, later food from little jars, and one day she drank from a cup. I gave her naps. I took her out for walks in her carriage.

All this may sound calm and matronly, but I was neither, and for me these acts were huge. I never knew from day to day what would happen or exactly what I was supposed to do about it, and I was alone to decide, except for the constant presence of

Dr. Spock, as carefully interpreted by me as the Torah has been by Jewish scholars. I read it so often that it became frayed with use. I kept looking for a paragraph that I'd somehow missed before or an extra meaning to the words that I'd already read. Joseph took part in all of this when he was home, but he wasn't home most of the time. At her bedtime, I couldn't decide on the exact place to put her blanket. Too low, she wouldn't be warm enough. Too high, she would smother. Turn her over? Not turn her over? I was a mess. The first time that she turned over by herself onto her back during a nap, I kept going into her room every few minutes, hanging over the crib, wondering anxiously if I should turn her back. It took three days for her to turn back it by herself. During those endless hours, I would pick her up, put her down. What did I *know*?

It wasn't all high anxiety, of course. There were many hours in between these fraught moments when we just did what we did. I tended her, and she gave me her need, her attention, her distress, or her pleasure. I learned. In the process, our love grew. We became a couple and with her father a threesome. She was beautiful and smart. I talked to her endlessly. And she, well, even though she couldn't talk, she could answer: with her eyes, her smile or tears, her intense attention. Walking with Alexandra in her stroller and her proud father in the Norfolk Azalea Gardens was a special time: the baby eagerly holding out her hands to the bright blooms everywhere and people stopping to comment, "How beautiful she is!"

The constant edge of worry and being off-balance informed the overwhelming responsibility, side by side with the passionate attachment growing with every day. Two sides of the same coin in this all-consuming relationship. In this way I became a mother. That is, "mother" was now me. No matter those absent dolls. I was now joined to this other person and she to me. Whatever life was and would become, it meant the two of us.

She had a father, and I was lucky enough that this particular father loved her with his own passion and cared for her from the start, whenever he could. His belief that he could and would do this was what enabled me to go to graduate school three years later, even as he did when his stint in the navy was over. So what if he called it "babysitting": he was still there in a way that most men, especially of our generation, were not. Our love for one another grew stronger. The baby didn't get in the way, as is often the case, because he wanted her so much and gave me as much support as he could.

Only, only—as much as this motherhood now defined me, it deprived me, and I knew it. Suzy Juhasz was not Suzy Hecht, and I missed that girl who had been me all of my life until March 12, 1964. Not just because she didn't have another human being appended to her like an extra arm or leg, but because things that made Suzy Hecht herself had disappeared. What I am saying here is nothing new, not in 2014, but then, as feminists finally pointed out in the 1960s and 1970s, Betty Friedan's famous "problem that had no name" not only didn't have a name but was not understood to be a problem. So what that I didn't write or act or dance or even *think* very much about anything besides my family and home? This was considered normal. Except of course, the urge to do these things was still inside me, whispering in a little voice that I could only just hear.

Why did I persist in creating a career, when so many women did not? Certainly not simply because I knew myself to be a smart and talented person. So were plenty of women. But culture told us, as it had told my own mother, that marriage/motherhood was our destiny in life. I went to graduate school because my husband wanted to go to graduate school. It was that simple. But graduate school radicalized me, and I am not referring to the national political movement that was happening at the very same time in Berkeley in the 1960s (though that mattered enormously to me, as well). I was turned on by thinking itself, which was happening at Berkeley in a way that I had never experienced before. My teachers constantly amazed me with how they worked with their minds. And here for the first time, my own intelligence was given a real opportunity to stretch and develop. It felt good. As I moved through the MA and PhD Programs, the idea of doing academic work myself as a career began to stir.

In 1971 I discovered feminism, which gave me the understanding that my goals made sense and that I was not alone in what had become a struggle. But although the beginnings of my graduate career in 1965 were in fact contiguous with the beginnings of second-wave feminism, I didn't know that then. My own introduction to feminism came later.

When Joseph talked about graduate school after the navy, which was always in his life plan, I slowly began to think, "Maybe I'll go, too." I'd never considered it before. Bennington girls weren't encouraged in scholarly matters. Our education had nothing to do with further education or careers, unless we tried out something in the arts. My own ambition had been to be an actor and a poet. But there I was in Norfolk—no acting, no writing. Just diapers and vacuum cleaners.

"School," I thought. "Maybe I'll be able to write poetry again there." Anyway, I liked school. I thought maybe I'd get a master's degree in English. No professional goals were attached to this idea then. It just meant doing something meaningful, interesting, and in the process hopefully writing poetry again. We applied to all the universities that interested him, and we both were accepted at Berkeley. I didn't have much say in the matter. I was pretty much going along for the ride. Childcare? That was an entirely fuzzy idea. We'd never had it, of course; I didn't know how you got it. But that would take care of itself, we imagined.

As we set off for California in the summer of 1965, the thought that was foremost in our minds was getting out of the navy. The Vietnam War was upon us, and Joseph knew that very soon the navy wouldn't let anyone go, no matter that his tour of duty was up. We had already decided that if this happened, he would declare himself a conscientious objector. But that would mean prison, not graduate school.

Luckily, we made it. We arrived in Berkeley, and it felt as if we had entered the promised land. Bell bottoms and long hair on everyone. Shops on Telegraph Avenue that sold pipes and bongs. Musicians in the streets. And huge bookstores, Cody's and Moe's. This had to be heaven. It certainly wasn't Kansas—or Norfolk. Pretty soon we had a used VW bug and were ensconced in student housing. But how would we care for Alexandra? Joseph and I needed to invent our own means by which a woman who was a mother could be a full-time graduate student, for we knew no models for these aspirations. Day care was not an idea then, much less a reality. But in the communal courtyard, we met Jackie, a "student wife" from Oklahoma with two kids, whose engineer husband had returned to school for his PhD. She agreed to care for thirteen-month-old Alexandra when I was in class. Joseph and I would trade off the rest of the time. Later, our arrangement for childcare turned into twenty hours a week.

Enter my old friend guilt. At first, it was enormous. Guilt, which would become a motif in my lifelong experience of motherhood, warring with those other powerful emotions, love and ambition. How could I leave my child with a stranger? How could I leave my child period? But oh, I loved classes. I'd never known such brilliant people as my professors. Of course I was intimidated, the little yokel from Bennington College, who didn't know half the terms for talking about literature that were tossed off so easily in my classes: "textuality," "pathetic fallacy," "trope," "objective correlative." But slowly I learned to hold my own— without using those words. Meanwhile Alexandra grew to love Jackie, a warm, maternal woman who sewed and baked pies and had love to spare for my little girl as well as her own children. We were lucky to have found her, and I learned something new about mothering: I could share it.

I was jealous of the other students, those who did not have to orchestrate their time so carefully: so many hours for class and study, so many hours to care for child and home. But in fact, this regimen was actually why I finished my degree in five years instead of the usual eight or nine. I was on a tight schedule. Sometimes, when I'd arrive home after an intense seminar session where the discussion had grown more and more abstract and less and less related to the text in hand, and I'd see the child needing to be fed or the dishes needing to be washed, the immediacy and tangibility of the life that awaited me made me feel lucky. Not that I didn't love all that wordplay, but I was in fact glad to be grounded again. My two worlds were difficult to manage, but they created a kind of balance, too.

When I entered graduate school, I had one daughter. Three years later I gave birth to another for my MA, and three years later a third for my PhD. Once we'd started a family, it didn't make sense to stop for the years that it would take me to get my degree. It turned out that at Berkeley, a master's was the degree that they gave to people who failed entrance to the PhD program, and I've never liked to fail at anything, even though it took me two go-rounds with the MA oral exam to get there. (I didn't know then that the professors often failed women students at the MA level: they didn't want us to go on for the PhD, because, they said, women would only get married and leave.) After my first failed exam, I stayed in bed for two days, afraid to face the world. But then I picked myself up and studied harder. I was eight months pregnant when I took the exam for the second time. Sometimes I think that the committee was afraid to fail me: what if I went into labor?

My MA daughter was Jenny, born in 1967 in the Summer of Love. By then we were out of student housing and living in the top-floor apartment of a beautiful Berkeley brown shingle house. There Alexandra learned to swing all by herself in the backyard. Our downstairs neighbor became Alexandra's babysitter, and when the new baby was born, my own sister Kathy stepped in to be the "nanny." Kathy's husband was now in the army, stationed at Fort Ord in nearby Oakland, for the Vietnam War had come.

This baby did have to be fed on a schedule. My mother still wasn't pleased, because the schedule was brought about by my being in graduate school and a mother, too: something of which she heartily disapproved. Jenny would not accept any fluid other than breast milk (not soy milk, not goat milk), so I'd feed her before I left for the university, come home at lunch for another feeding, and then again when I returned at four. Her favorite time each day—and mine, too, really—was my bedtime, when she'd always wake, and we could nurse as long as she wanted. Long after she'd learned to drink milk from a cup during the rest of the day, she kept our evening rendezvous: sleepy and warm in the covers, just for us.

Antonia, my PhD daughter, was born in 1970. By that time we were at Bucknell University, where Joseph was a new assistant professor of psychology, and I'd been finishing my dissertation on metaphor in modern long poems, struggling to turn it in before my baby came. Unlike the speedy arrival of Jenny, Antonia's birth was an altogether different experience. The doctor decided to induce her a week early because he was scheduled for a golfing holiday. This early birth proved long and worthy of the word "labor."

But in the hospital in Lewisburg something more frightening occurred: I contracted double strep pneumonia. The symptoms did not emerge until two weeks later, and Joseph was wise enough to drive me—gasping for breath, in terrible pain—to the nearby town of Danville, where Geisinger Hospital, modeled after the Mayo Clinic, was located. They saved my life. I was there for three weeks. Despite my precarious situation, I pumped my breasts, which shocked the hospital staff. My baby was not allowed in the hospital, nor were my other children, so they would come to the parking lot, while I would stand at the window with tears running down my cheeks, and this was how we visited. The sobbing was not good for my lungs, but I could not stop.

When I came home at last, Antonia was a bottle baby. She wasn't very interested in breasts, and so for days, she and I seemed to be nursing around the clock, until she was finally used to it and could get enough milk. Still, she weaned herself to the cup early at six months, an independent soul who has remained so till this day.

So, motherhood…with my second and third daughters, things were different from those lonely frightened days in faraway Virginia. I knew something about babies then. One thing I knew was that I now loved them as a breed. I really liked being pregnant. I liked letting my body take over and turn me into a physical being. Giving birth was an experience close to ecstasy, a high that was greater than any psychedelic drug could induce, no matter the pain, or maybe pain was a part of the altering of consciousness. Nursing came in a close second. The sheer joy of that body encircled by mine, those trusting eyes looking up at me. Overall, it turned out that aiding a small person to grow and flower into herself, despite all of the difficulties involved, was worth pretty much everything.

Alexandra was a lively, intense little girl whose bright eyes reflected her strong spirit and endless energy. She has remained this person all of her life, morphing into a skinny kid whose long straggly hair dipped over the books that she was always reading, a suddenly tall teenager who bossed her sisters around, ran the year book, swam on the swim team, got straight As, was a member of the first women's class at Amherst College.

Then came Jenny, with her sweet brown eyes and beloved rag of a blanket called "Blablie": small, stubborn, determined, perfectionist child who became a gymnast at eight and rose to stardom until felled by a shattered elbow in her teens. But later she became a modern dancer at Brown University.

Last was Antonia, with her slanty "Hungarian" eyes and curly dark hair: willful as a child and then a rebellious teenager who did or didn't do things her way, the little sister who became the most independent of them all. Her interest in left-wing politics was alive even in high school, and at Brown (like her sister before her), she majored in public policy.

The shelves on my bookcase are filled with photo albums that document the moments of their rich, delightful childhood lives. I remember Alex carefully meting out the Halloween candy to her sisters, so many per night, with her pal Wendy creating outrageous satiric performances a la *Saturday Night Live* for their families. Jenny in her nightgown sitting on the floor heater, eating sunflower seeds, studying into the night. Jenny on the balance beam, such intense concentration focused in her small, strong body. Toni the jazz dancer, in top hat and tights, and her high-school research paper on Elizabeth Cady Stanton that sowed the seeds for future activism.

Years of family, as it grew and circled and moved in different directions, but always around an abiding center. Whatever else complicated our lives, family love was strong.

Although I had been living in Berkeley during the late 1960s, when feminism was taking over that radical community, I didn't pay much attention. For one thing, I was too busy, but for another, I didn't think that it had anything to do with me. Didn't I have it all? My early struggles around my own identity as a mother had been embryonic, personal. I considered that my mother/scholar balancing act in graduate school for five years was equally personal, for I had taken on an untraditional challenge. There were few women studying for the PhD at Berkeley in the 1960s, and none that I knew had children. In fact, there was only one woman on the faculty there, and she was unmarried and childless.

I was lucky. My husband gave me support and encouragement, and so did my mentor, Josephine Miles, who was that one unmarried and childless professor.

But when I went out with my new Berkeley PhD to get a job, I was defeated at every turn for five years. Schools "lost" my application. They didn't reply when I answered their ads. When I had an interview, they didn't hire me. At Bucknell, where Joseph was an assistant professor, they gave me a part-time instructorship but no more: the chairman told me it was because I was a "faculty wife." "We used to have to hire wives, but things are better for us now," he said. I heard these words, but they didn't make sense. Throughout this period, I thought that I simply wasn't good enough.

My aha moment came in 1971. The children were eight, five, and two. Two were in grammar school. One was being cared for by a young couple: he was a graduate student. Day care, finally a reality, had not made it to Lewisburg, Pennsylvania. One afternoon I was standing in the Bucknell library in the New Books section, in my miniskirt, tights, and high boots. I saw a book entitled *American Women and American Studies*, by Betty E. Chmaj, published in 1971 by the Women's Free Press. American Studies is an interdisciplinary field that includes English along with history, philosophy, and other humanities, so I figured that I was included. That book literally changed my life. Chmaj had interviewed women academics at all stages of their careers. As I leafed through the pages, I started to cry, for what I read was so painful. I had to find a corner where I could sit down.

No real expectations for me as a future scholar—assumption that I did not really "need" a job because I was married. (2)

Last job: not considered for full time position, though professionally qualified. Placed on lower rank and salary. (3)

It wasn't marriage so much as having children that hurt me with the fellowship people . . . When I was told why, I was dumfounded. (2)

We have moved twice. The college my husband is now located at has an unspoken and unwritten rule against nepotism. The other colleges nearby are reducing their departments because of the economic situation. I keep up in my field, have published one article and am working on another, just in case there is an opening. My husband is extremely sympathetic. I realize I am not the only woman who is trained and educated forced to stay home because she is married. I feel hopeless and really don't know what to do. (4)

Chmaj comments on the difficulties with promotion and tenure for women: "Women are generally in the bottom ranks . . . If promotion happens at all, they also wait longer from PhD to first promotion, and from first promotion to second."

She also gave a questionnaire to the women, asking them about their emotional responses to academic treatment. The total vote of eighty-four responded to these choices: self-doubt, 13; humiliation, 9; rage, 38; confusion, 9; powerless, 12; helplessness, 12.

When I read these words in 1971, I was shocked. Shocked at my own ignorance, shocked at the brutality systematically imbedded in my chosen profession, and most of all shocked to discover that my story did not really have much to do with me personally. Over and over I read my own experiences described, and I learned about the future spreading out before me, a future that I'd never even thought about, so intent was I on step one. Suddenly I saw myself as not alone but rather belonging to something that one would have to call, for what other word was there, a sisterhood. The fault for this treatment did not lie with me or with any of these women. There actually was something lethal in the culture, the thing that they called sexism. My mind tumbled all over itself as it tried to rearrange so many of my ideas about how I understood myself and the world in which I lived.

Suddenly possessing what is called a political analysis, sensing a belonging with my fellow women academics instead of the competitiveness that I had learned so well in graduate school, and realizing that there were wrongs in the academic world that needed to be changed was overwhelming. I had become a feminist.

(Now, when I read these stories, I am shocked all over again, because many of those facts are still true for academic women today. I find it horrifying.)

This is how feminism entered my life, but what did it have to do with motherhood? Everything. Because if feminism taught me that women, especially married women, especially women with children, had a particularly difficult time in my profession, it also taught me, especially by way of the small "consciousness-raising" groups of women meeting in living rooms everywhere and subsequently my own, that I had a right to be a mother who worked at a profession. In my group we told our stories, week after week, and we gave one another support if not much information as to *how* to do it, for we were, as they say, "flying by the seat of our pants."

How did one teach the courses, attend the meetings, do the research and writing necessary for promotion, *and* raise the children? How did one do two jobs at the same time, especially when both of them required 24/7 immersion? We didn't know, but we wanted to try.

First of all, childcare was needed, but in my life, there were no childcare centers until Antonia was a small child. We had to find helpers on our own. Between Joseph and myself, we never arranged for more than twenty hours of help, because we felt that it was wrong. "Wrong" is the significant word here, for we believed that we must never short-change our children on behalf of our professions. And yet, no matter Joseph's wholehearted desire to be a fully responsible parent, so rare for the time, our situations were not the same. Quite simply, he was expected to work, and I was not.

Feminism may have encouraged us to persist in finding academic jobs, but when I began to teach at last, I was in a man's field. To stay there, I had to show that I could do the job just as well as the men around me—that is, that I could do it their way. "Their way" meant that I must never act like a stereotypical woman: never show weakness or be emotional and especially never cry (only in the ladies' room). Later I began to have ideas about how I wanted to do the work but in a way that differed from the traditional format. In the beginning, however, I just wanted to stay, and I understood something even more fundamental: that having a child must not interfere with anything required of me. In fact, it was best if no one knew that I was a mother, for if my "colleagues" had children, they had wives who cared for them, and the children had nothing to do with their work.

I remember sitting around a conference table and suddenly milk beginning to seep onto my blouse, for the meeting had run longer than expected, and it was past time for me to rush home for feeding time. I tried to cover my shame with my sweater. But I worried a lot about the after-effects of this transgression.

In the years that followed, there were actually enough feminists in the profession to join one another, to organize and try to address those practices described in Chmaj's book that made it so hard for women to work as academics: issues concerned with hiring, promotion, and equal pay. But when I started, I was one of three women in the English department, and the other two were unmarried and childless. In the beginning, trying to combine motherhood and my desire to *be* an academic was my driving concern.

Joseph and I continued to find people willing to help us to care for our children, especially before they went to school. Jackie in Berkeley, Cindy in Lewisburg, and Sheila in New Zealand. Loving people, each very different from the two of us. A good thing, something that children in other cultures in extended families know well. But it came with their knowledge that I was not always available to them. How much brings independence and how much brings insecurity? When Antonia was little, day care had finally been invented. "Good," we said. But when I wanted to start her in Saturday ballet class when she was four, as I had done for the others, she said, "No!" She was the best and most instinctive little dancer of them all. I knew it from waltzing around the living room with her, so I insisted. On the day of her first class, she walked into the studio—and peed on the floor. That showed me. She wanted the pleasure of being at home on the weekends.

The girls grew older; they went to school. They were good students, with friends and activities. They knew that they were deeply loved by their parents. But then my guilt took a new form. They were a part of the outside world now. The norms of the culture were affecting them as well as me. They knew "normal" mothers who did not employ daytime babysitters or send their children to daycare. Mothers who participated in bake sales for the gymnastic team. Mothers who showed up at every school event. Mothers like they saw on TV: *Brady Bunch* mothers.

Feminism had taught me that I shouldn't feel guilty if I was not home baking cookies when the children returned from school and I was teaching a class. I was okay about the cookies, but not so much when I missed a swim meet or a school event.

Now I think that I was more adamant about the things that I refused to do because I was so unsure of what I *could* do and still succeed at work. I had no guidelines. The more that I tried to be true to my code—not to give up at the university, to publish, to become an associate professor and then a full professor—the more I think that I overdid my notions of what was not possible or necessary for a mother to do, and consequently, the guiltier I felt about these decisions.

I am still haunted by the nots. Not showing up at a school play when Alex thought that I was there. Not picking Jenny up at the airport when her gymnastics team returned from an out-of-state meet (I was divorced by then) and asking her, when she called in tears wanting to know where I was, to get a ride with someone else. I'd assumed that because she drove with others to the airport when they departed that a ride back was also part of the arrangement. But still. How could I?

Today, Alex doesn't remember this event or says she doesn't. Jenny remembers, but it has long since receded as a major moment in her childhood. But for me, these moments and others like them are still cause for shame. I put my work first so many times, no matter how much I loved my children. There was no way that I could be a "normal" mother, for normal mothers didn't have careers. In my efforts to deny the system, I think that I sometimes short-changed the girls.

This is what subsequent generations are responding to, I know. The issue of how best to raise children is very much alive—especially for women who work.

At my retirement party, that lovely event arranged by Jenny and attended by all of my daughters, each one spoke of seeing me as a role model: a woman who could succeed in a profession, a profession historically dominated by men, lighting the way for them and others to do so, too. I was thrilled. In truth, their remarks meant more to me than all the books that I have published. Each is a marvelous woman who has dealt with career and motherhood in different ways. Alex has followed my pattern. She has managed to be a brilliant and successful professor of media studies and a loving mother of two. Jenny, with her PhD in psychology, has chosen part-time employment as an instructor so as to involve herself more fully and creatively in her children's lives. Antonia, after graduate work in public policy, is a well-known journalist and public speaker; she doesn't have children at present. Feminists all. Books that they have written sit on my shelves along with their childhood photos. Choice and chance have shaped their lives, in addition to the cultural milieu that defines these times, so different from the 1960s and 1970s in which they grew up.

Today many educated middle-class women younger than my daughters are opting out of the professional world to be full-time mothers. They say that trying to do two jobs at once is impossible—and bad for the children. They think that their jobs will wait for them. I wish that it were so simple, but that isn't usually the case. To me, as a 1970s feminist, after all our work and struggle to achieve affirmative action, equal pay for women, childcare, and other less overt issues—no matter that our efforts were not 100 percent successful—this is so sad. They don't even realize that they speak with the heritage of our work as their cushion, that we had to win for them their very assumption that they are entitled to the professions that they so cavalierly relinquish. Perhaps some of this, ironically, is made possible by our feminist revolution.

I am now the mother of adult women, and my memories of how I came to be a mother and how I mothered my three daughters forms the fret of experience that informs my present maternal identity. At a time when professional women mothers were an oddity, I managed to get a PhD and then become a full professor of English. There were many barriers to achieving these goals, but I had support: from my husband, who encouraged my studies and my work, and from other women all along the way. My feminist beliefs and the strength of my love for my children were in some ways the most important support, for feminism taught me that I could and should do this, and I needed to be my best self to be the best kind of mother that my children deserved.

They were babies, little girls, young women, and adults. They are my greatest treasure. But I could not have been me, the woman who raised them, if I had not worked at a job, as well. I was and am all the richer as a human being for it, yet I know that this attempt to occupy what was seen as a competing world was not simple, causing me to make mistakes, even as it allowed me to offer them gifts.

7

Grandmotherhood

If they're lucky, mothers turn into grandmothers. Grandmothers who are mothers of daughters have daughters who are mothers. This is a particularly complicated weave. Grandmothers have grandchildren, but they continue to be mothers, and so the nature of that relationship turns once again. When Emma Sadie Juhasz Schwartz was born in 1997, my life grew simultaneously richer and more complex.

Emma is Jenny's daughter. Her birth was followed by the arrival of Alex's daughter Simone Irene Dunye in 1998, Alex's son Gabriel James Robert Juhasz in 2001, and Jenny's second daughter Eliza Sadie Juhasz Schwartz in 2001.

Their births were astonishing, beautiful, overwhelming in every way: so much new love for a person suddenly arriving in the world. Simultaneously, there was a widening and shifting of love for my own girls.

Grandmothers immediately step into a cultural frame (in my case, for American, middle-class, white women), an image that hasn't changed very much in the twentieth- or twenty-first century, as far as I can tell. Grandmother—a white-haired lady with a wide lap and an endless supply of fresh-baked cookies: comfy, nurturing, always on call, smothering her grandchildren with goodies and doting love.

As new feminists in the 1970s, I and my cohorts in our consciousness-raising groups, with our poems and novels and essays, mapped the outlines for what we considered our rights as women. However, we didn't think much about grandmothers; why would we? For one thing, we were young; for another, the idea of motherhood was daunting enough. In our memories, or myths, which tended to inform one another, our mothers were the problem, while grandmothers were imagined as a source of comfort and even inspiration. It was okay for grandmothers to knit and bake those cookies. When our mothers did this, however, we said that they'd sold out to the patriarchy. And so, as the years passed, while nonfeminist mothers followed in their mothers' footsteps and feminist mothers struggled with their own triumphs and demons to do it differently, grandmothers were left to be what they "always" were.

When I became a grandmother eighteen years ago, I never gave a thought to stereotypes. I just moved happily into the whirl of excitement and expanding love that the arrival of these babies occasioned. For a good many years, as each child was born and grew into toddlerhood and small childhood, there was a role and a need for me that, I discovered, had as much to do with my motherhood as my grandmotherhood. That need gave me a new place in my daughters' lives. For no woman has been the mother of daughters without experiencing that intense tug between closeness and separating that is a hallmark of this relationship. For a while suspicion and criticism seemed to have been usurped by something purer and more elemental: a daughter who is a new mother wants and needs her own mother to help with the magic and work of mothering. That simple. No, not simple at all, but real. Babies give the whole family a center for care.

But babies turn into toddlers, toddlers into kids, kids into preteens, and preteens into teens. Relationships swirl and change, but stereotypes don't. Now when the simple caretaking for small children in our lives has not been primary for a long time, I look back on those early days with yearning as well as joy. They don't last. The need for primary care morphs into different forms. For toddlers and kids, there is "babysitting": the meals that are cooked, the games that are played, the stories that are read, the bedtime rituals and school pickups. But then acts such as these become less needed, too. For me there have been other forms of grandmothering, such as doing activities together and carefully chosen gifts. But the white-haired old lady with the cookie jar still looks out from the pages of grandmother.com and does not approve of these substitutes.

When I think of what I meant to Emma when she was little and what I mean to her now, I am sad. I love her in all of her blooming womanhood, but whereas once I was her special person, now I am simply a member of her extended family. I am Grammy. Am I special? Certainly not in the way that I was for many years. I am there, as I have always been there. I don't think that this is a story simply about Emma and me. I think it's a story about aging: mine and hers. I mention Emma because she is the oldest. I have a different relationship with her younger sister, Eliza, and with each of my grandchildren who live in another city, Gabe and Simone. But the process seems the same: change.

My experience is not just personal, I believe. It is also, or at the same time, a story about stereotypes for women in my culture. "Grandmother." One problem with stereotypes, like "grandmother," is that they do their work both from the outside of people and within them. When I was first a grandmother, adopting the cultural image of grandmother seemed simple and natural. I wanted to be that person with the wide lap—nurturing and always on call; both I and my daughters were comfortable in our roles. As life moved on, however, as caretaking of babies and young children became less central to our lives and my time with my grandchildren grew shorter, I often felt guilt. Was I shirking? Was I still a good grandmother? Did my daughters think so?

From my vantage point as a woman in her seventies who is the grandmother of teenagers, I am able to see more of the journey that my daughters, my grandchildren, and I have taken. I can see now that there are stages to grandmothering, as there are to any other role that we are given or assume for the long haul, and that any stereotype that remains unidimensional is as harmful as it is useless. When I read grandmother.com, the only changes for the traditional role of grandmothers that I can find there are a few essays about how grandmothers are younger now, so we can still be groovy. There is nothing that takes into account stages in grandmothering. The evolution that I personally have experienced in my identity as grandmother, affecting both my grandchildren and my daughters, has evolved from the traditional role but is more complicated. I mean the mix between what I could and could not do; what my daughters wanted from me and what they needed from me, along with what they did not want or need; and finally what the children themselves wanted and/or needed changed over and over.

I might have done some things differently, and I might have done some things beautifully, but again, as with mothering, I can see how my daughters and I all have struggled with our sense of what was "expected" along with what actually happened. Most importantly, however, I look back on that journey with the knowledge that today as then we are a loving family. The story, now eighteen years of it, will tell the tale.

Jenny sitting in the blue-and-white striped rocking chair, cradling one-day-old Emma, a bundle in a cotton blanket. We arrive: with me are Joseph; Christina and Linda, his two small daughters from his second marriage; and Paul, Jenny's husband, who has picked us up at the airport. The expression on her face is a mixture of pride, love, fear, unease, and joy; it brings quick tears to my eyes. My daughter, a mother! Her baby, the tiny smidge of a face peering out from the blanket, seems beautiful beyond belief. We all rush to Jenny, wanting to kiss her—and to hold the baby. At once gratefully and reluctantly, she hands tiny Emma to me. And I am a grandmother.

Our airline tickets are for a one-week stay. In warm, sweet-smelling Decatur, Georgia, we help to rock and bathe and endlessly admire the astonishing Emma, as Jenny and Paul begin the work that is now theirs for a lifetime: parenthood. We take her for walks around the neighborhood; we hold her when she cries or when she doesn't. The week goes by in a flash. Then one day, as our visit draws to a close, Jenny takes me aside and asks if I can stay on for another week if possible. She tells me that it's all too scary, not knowing what will happen next. Of course I understand, having been in this very place myself. And I was only twenty-two, even younger than Jenny, who is twenty-four. My daughter needs me; I am delighted to change my reservations.

The second week is even more special. No longer a crowd in the house but a little family: me included. When Emma cries at night and can't be soothed, Jenny and Paul often put her into her car seat and drive around the neighborhood to calm her, a time-honored tactic that really works. I always hear them leaving the house, then returning, as there is no door to the room where I sleep. One morning, after they've all come home in the wee hours, I hear Emma wake, while her parents sleep the sleep of the just. Knowing that she's recently been fed, I decide to pick her up and try to quiet her myself so that they can keep sleeping. I tiptoe into Emma's room, pick her up and swathe her, and take her out to the backyard. I walk her to and fro and sing to her. The garden is lush, and the birds chirp. It's summer; it's Georgia; even at this early hour, it's already warm. After a while, lo and behold, she settles snugly into my arms and peacefully sleeps. I can tend both this infant and my own daughter. I *am* a good grandmother.

The day comes when I must leave all three to their own life. It's time; we know. But it's a scary moment for everyone. We've come to depend on one another, and now the little family must form its own nucleus. Jenny cries; I cry. I know that it has helped Jenny to have me right there to give advice as well as assistance. I like to be this person, and it feels so wonderful to have my daughter this close to me again. But even as I sent her off to college far away, now I am the one to leave, because I must. Naturally, in the days that follow, they do just fine, and their child flourishes, as can be seen in the countless photographs and videos that document the wonders of this first baby. But still, we had those days, the four of us *and* the two of us, Emma and me.

Simone is the next grandchild to be born, three years later, in a rented hillside house in Los Angeles. She is eight weeks early. Simone is the biological child of Cheryl, Alex's partner. Each woman has decided to bear a child, and so they will make a family with, as the cliché goes, "two mommies." Cheryl became pregnant first, but this birth has become sudden and frightening. In March she has gone to the hospital with heart failure, where it is discovered that she has hyperthyroid disease that had gone undetected, masked by signs of pregnancy. She begins to recover, but suddenly there is a premature baby, meant to be born in May, and the new home that they were readying for their child is still being restored. Plus, they are right in the middle of packing up the old one.

To complicate matters further, Simone is sent home six days after her birth! I arrive with Joseph and his girls, now fourteen and twelve. We will be the team, packing and painting, with Alex as commander-in-chief, and I will help with Simone, that tiny girl with no fat on her anywhere. A little chicken, we call her. There she lies in her bassinette, right in the middle of the living room. Because of all the work that must be done before the new house is ready, I frequently tend Simone, my baby-skills honed from the birth of Emma two years before, while the others work around me or at the house in nearby Pasadena. I can give her the bottles that we use to supplement Cheryl's breastfeeding, and I can rock and sing and coo. Cheryl, even as she recovers, cooks big meals for everyone. It is a huge enterprise, but we are all in it together, and things are getting done. Simone is plumping up a little. Alex is our general, as we pack, unpack, and work on the house itself. I may be the only one who can tell how anxious she is underneath it all. Knowing this, I can offer little kindnesses as well as push myself a little harder to do the tasks that arise: my way, this time around, of caring for her as well as for Simone.

Alex and Cheryl will always be more cavalier about child-rearing than Jenny and Paul could dream of being. This very week, in the middle of everything, we all go *bowling*! Simone comes, too: in her carry seat, with a receiving blanket draped loosely over the handle to "protect her from germs." My motherly/grandmotherly heart is aflutter. This can't be right, I tell myself fearfully and count the minutes until we can leave.

But in the end, everyone survives nicely. Simone grows healthy and strong, until after a year, as promised, you can't even tell that she'd been premature. Cheryl recovers rapidly. The lovely new house is finished, and the move takes place in a matter of weeks. Alex becomes a doting mother to Simone. The "Crazy Week" becomes the centerpiece of the lore surrounding Simone's birth.

Alex's son Gabriel is born a mere year and a half later. Both children have the same father, so they are truly sister and brother. The baby is due on July 14, Bastille Day, but Alex has been having contractions for two weeks now. Breathless phone calls punctuate my evenings. But every time, the contractions disappear by the next day. Finally, a few days before the due date, I can't take it anymore. "I'm coming!" I say. I arrive on July 12, and then at least we all get to wait together. July 14 comes and goes. Alex is getting huge, hot, and tired. We walk to the park with Simone; we walk home again. Another dinner. Another night. This feels like forever, but actually, it's just two days. On July 16, on the way home from the park in the afternoon, Alex gets another contraction so strong that she has to stop and hold on to a tree. But then it's gone, and another one doesn't follow. She laughs ruefully, and home we go. Finally, however, the contractions just keep on coming, and they *decide*: we're going to the hospital!

My job is to stay with sleeping Simone, lie by the phone with my heart beating madly and wait. So that's what I do. And do. And do. Finally the phone rings, and it's Cheryl to tell me that yes, the baby really is coming. But there was meconium in the fluid when Alex's water broke, indicating possible fetal distress. The baby's heartbeat is irregular and needs to be monitored. This is just precautionary: everything is probably all right. Probably all right! Terrified, I lie in bed by the phone. Of course I don't sleep: what I do is pray. Me, who is not traditionally religious and doesn't do this sort of thing on a regular basis. But it comes as a matter of course. As in, what else would one do? Sometime before dawn, the second call comes at last. All is well. Alex is fine, and her brand-new son, Gabriel, is fine, too. My heart continues to pump at a rapid pace—with relief now and a fierce joy.

In the hospital, I see my firstborn with her beautiful son in her arms, a radiant, tender smile infusing her being. Alex has changed overnight from one kind of beauty (tough, cool, savvy) to another: gentle and shining. I am slave to them both. This state continues for the two weeks that I stay in Pasadena. I didn't expect that this daughter, too, my super-independent, always-in-control eldest child, would ask me to extend my originally scheduled one-week visit. But in these early days we have worked as a team, and she, like her sister before her, feels the need of more time with a mother alongside. Surely it's the newness of motherhood that has brought out this need in both of them, generally so busy with their lives that I tend to sit on the sidelines. But I also wonder, in retrospect, if assuming the mother part of a mother-child relationship sparks a renewed interest in having a mother.

It's a different household here in Pasadena with a more hectic style, especially with a jealous toddler to care for, as well. I take Simone to the park to give her some time for herself. I give Alex respite when I can. She doesn't want much—she adores tending to her child—but there are still moments for me to change Gabe to the tinkling of the little musical bunny that I brought and, best of all, to dance with him to old rock 'n' roll tunes. Sometimes Alex and I go to the park with both children in the double stroller, and I swing with each one. At home it's open house to well-wishers, so I do a lot of dishes—but I gloat over that, too. It's another way to share in the happiness that is Alex and Gabe.

A few months later, in November, it's time for Jenny's second daughter Eliza to be born. No airplanes for me this time. Jenny and her little family moved back to Boulder when Emma was two years old! They lived in my finished basement that summer while they were house hunting. Imagine. I never thought that any of my children would return to Boulder. I always pictured myself moving to one of their cities after I retired. They came because I was here and Jenny's father was here, along with his daughters. They came for family—and help, since her lawyer husband Paul is a litigator and she is a psychologist. "Whatever," I thought. "They're here."

This time around, I get it all. To have Jenny tell me shyly over lunch one day that she is pregnant again. To be there in person to watch her pregnancy bloom. And to be called the night that they decide it's time to go to the hospital. So one more time I lie by the phone, while Emma sleeps across the hall. I do *not* sleep. Not much later (it seems like forever) the call comes. Eliza is born: she has arrived very quickly. I give Emma her breakfast, and then Paul comes and takes her to the hospital. I arrive later, greeted by all four of them, Jenny, Paul, Emma, and Eliza, in the hospital bed, arms around one another, with Jenny gently sleeping. Soon I hold the tiny, winsome dark-haired Eliza, only a few hours old.

That night is a first. Emma comes to our house for dinner and to sleep overnight. She's never slept away from her parents before, so everyone is a little nervous. But it goes swimmingly. The Sara Lee chocolate cake that I serve that night, resurrected memory from my own childhood, becomes a staple of many "dinner parties" to follow.

Thus the pattern is set for Eliza's early days. My part is to care for both children: sing Eliza to sleep, take Emma to the chilly park. It's November, so we play wild running games to keep warm. Later, after Jenny has returned to her volunteer work at the Boulder County AIDS Project, I bundle Eliza into the car and drive her down to BCAP so that Jenny can nurse her between clients. As time passes, I will sit for Liza, then take her off to Flatirons School, where together we pick up Emma from kindergarten. We arrive a little early, to get in a swing or two in the school playground. And so it goes. Surely I am the luckiest grandmother in Boulder: central to the heartbeat of this family.

I delight in writing these vignettes, early memories of babies being born to my daughters, as we all were discovering that most primary of human experiences: birth itself. Despite the fears that accompanied these moments, the surge of love itself was so central that behavior seemed to know where to go. Love for the child and for one another is a powerful directive. The tales that I tell show me behaving in traditional grandmother fashion. I am a caregiver: to my grandchild, my daughter, and her family. What I did felt right, and far from questioning it, I was exalted by it.

Childcare remains central for a long time. This is good, if only because the love relationship between grandmother and baby and grandmother and toddler is special and new. Actually, for a long time I felt less like a caregiver than a lover. I was in a state of adoration for each child. Anecdotal writing that I have read about contemporary grandmotherhood nearly always refers to this sudden passion. Later, as the babies grew into toddlers, a two-way love affair began for me that in some ways was even more remarkable, after the lifetime of hedged bets that had character-ized daughter/mother love for me. First I fell in love with those tiny infants. Then this big love was actually returned. Suddenly, I turned into Glinda the Good Witch or maybe Cinderella's Fairy Godmother. At the sight of me, their faces would light up with delight. To them I was quite simply and unconditionally wonder-ful. The first few times that this happened, I turned my head to see who they were looking at. Imagine seeing a toddler's eyes brighten when I entered the room; hearing this child chortle with pleasure, as if a great gift had been given to her or to him!

When Emma was four, nothing was more exciting than a "dinner party" and sleepover at Grammy's. She'd get all dressed up. Before dinner we'd pick flowers in my garden and put them in a wicker basket, and she would bring them proudly into the house. Emma liked "pink salmon fish." She also liked "Grammy's chicken," the very same cutlets that I had taught her mother to make. But they seemed to taste much better at my house. And always that Sara Lee chocolate cake for dessert. She'd eat the frosting and forget about the cake—but who cared?

As she grew a little older, the tradition of poem writing at the dinner table began. My partner Branny or I or Emma herself would offer a line, and then we would go around the table, each person adding another thought that would rhyme with the first, until the poem was finished. All of the poems were written with colored markers into a little blank book that I'd purchased especially for this purpose. One day Emma grew old enough to write down the words herself. (I still have the little book on my shelf.)

All of this was quite simply wonderful. Helping my daughters, spending time with my grandchildren felt good, and it helped someone else to feel good: because babies and little children *need* to be cared for; because I am a mother, and I know how to do this; because I was socialized as a female, and caregiving is at the top of the list for what, in cultural terms, makes a female "feminine." Even if I've challenged that role, as well as the very word "feminine" itself, I have reaped the rewards that caring brings. It brings gratitude, praise, and also acceptance. For a woman, caregiving is above cultural reproach.

Yet even at the start of my life as a grandmother, there were complications. They began first with the fallout that soon developed with respect to my *mother* role. For as I have said, becoming a grandmother does not erase one's motherhood, but it does modify it, a fact that usually gets swept under the rug. A grandmother continues to be a mother; you cannot simply bifurcate the two. A new mother is still a daughter, and in the beginning, both young women were in their way newborns, too, and needing their own mother. But soon they became more confident in their identities as mothers. As they became less dependent on me as guide and teacher, they began to establish their own maternal structures and rules. Much as I loved their original need for me, I loved watching them grow into devoted, creative mothers. My own problem with this situation was worry. Not about challenging but about breaking their rules—and as a consequence falling out of favor with *them*. For me the rules became a test of my grandmotherhood, which, in turn, became a test of my worth.

I remember sitting on a swing in Atlanta with ten-month-old Emma. On an outing to the park, I held her in my lap, swinging and singing. I made up a song just for her, and together we felt the rhythms of flying, even as we sat safely together. But suddenly I panicked. *Were* we safe? For I looked down and saw Emma's tiny arm pressed against the metal chains of the swing. There were red marks from the pressure! What had I done to her? Heart beating madly, I slowed the swing to a stop and took her to sit on a park bench, willing the marks to subside. She showed no sense of pain, but still. We were to be home in ten minutes, and my daughter Jenny did not tolerate lateness lightly. Emma was due for the next stage in her schedule. But the redness persisted.

What did I fear? That I had unwittingly hurt her. Would we have to rush her to the emergency room? But there was as well the fear that Jenny would be furious with me for having allowed this disaster to occur. Finally, there was no choice. I had to strap Emma into her stroller and push her home. Heart in mouth, I handed her into her mother's arms. Apologizing profusely, I showed her the marks on Emma's arm. Jenny looked, felt very carefully, and then pronounced, "This will be okay, Mom."

To complicate the matter, there were more than one set of rules. From the start it was clear that the two sisters had very different styles of mothering and that this was a bone of contention between them. Jenny's rules revolved around an intense concern for safety—and for decorum, as well. Alex was Jenny's opposite. She valued freedom above all for her children; she believed that they should be as unfettered as possible and was much more tolerant in the matter of danger. I, as their mother, did *not* take sides: that seemed the wisest solution in the situation. But that did not prevent me from worrying. With Alex I worried because I was concerned about both the lack of safety and of decorum; with Jenny I worried that I could not always live up to her standards for safety and decorum. During the times when we were all together in one group, well, the tension was thick, and I grew very quiet.

In ways such as these, this grandmothering turns out to be a new incarnation of the old struggle between mother and daughter. Is not daughterly criticism at the very heart of the mother-daughter relationship? Beginning with the earlier pull toward separate identity, a daughter so often sees her mother as incarnating all that she herself believes she is not or wishes not to be. As a mother of daughters, I have experienced full well the difficulties in discovering that you have become the person who is wrongness personified. For me, that old pain has never healed, no matter how much I understand it intellectually. So here it came again, under a new banner.

But now I think that the issue is even more intricate. I see that young mothers, whether they admit it, as I did, or not, are themselves worried about doing it right. In fact, they do continue to need their own mother's help. Perhaps the cultural grandmother fantasy persists because her capacity for care is so valued. But it is also constantly scrutinized. What if she actually doesn't know? What if she gets it wrong? Even though I viewed myself as completely different from my own mother, I had been through this experience before, when a grandmother did get it wrong.

What I knew was that the child's very safety is at stake, and the first rule of motherhood is to protect one's child at all costs. No matter (I really believe) that our situations were different from what I experienced as a young mother, it became clear to me that the grandmother, who is after all the mother's mother, serves as a ready and familiar target for blame. The old tug of closeness and distance between mother and daughter continues on in a new arena.

Between mother and daughter, yes. But it arises between grandmother and grandchild, too. Babies grow. They turn into toddlers and then into kids. How exciting. I think of them as children. Slender Emma with her dark hair and eyes, now intent and pensive, now sparkling with excitement, growing lovelier by the day. Gabriel with his sensitive face and flyaway hair, long skinny legs, and bright eyes telegraphing his latest plot for a joke or an invention. Simone, both thoughtful and wild, growing into her tall, beautiful body and awkwardly seeking her own special way. Eliza with her wicked grin, vibrant energy, and tiny, compact, strong body.

The children entered school, and their lives grew richer and fuller in their own sphere. There was a world of friends now: play dates and sleepovers with friends. After school, there were activities: soccer, gymnastics, ballet, singing, and acting. But of course, they were still children, and so their mother and father and siblings remained the center from which they would swing out and back. But I discovered that for me, grandmothers no longer had a central place at the hearth, and this was painful.

Part of the changes had to do with me. First of all, I had a demanding job. I was a full professor, and I couldn't always provide help exactly when it was needed. (I probably negotiated my work responsibilities more in the early days of grandmothering.) Although I participated in the pickups from preschool and grammar school for years, it's a fact that I don't like to drive in the snow, so later on, college-aged nannies did that job. I don't like to stay up late, either, so as the years passed, I became a last-ditch nighttime sitter. In different ways I crossed myself off some caregiver lists.

I have been speaking a great deal of my local grandchildren, but the difficulty was magnified with the two California kids. Ours has always been a long-distance relationship. I go there for visits; they come here for visits. I did this regularly at least twice a year—until my neck injury, along with the onslaught of my arthritis, started to prevent my frequent air travel. Now I do not go as much. This feels bad. When I'm there, I can participate in their daily lives. And I get to be with my daughter, which matters a lot. So not to visit in the old way has deprived me of much that I value and them of a better relationship with me.

When these kids were younger, I was always up for a walk to the park or to the small local Italian market. I brought presents. I would carefully search the shelves of Boulder stores to find just the right books that I imagined would please Gabie. And they did; only one day he announced, "Grammy, stop bringing books and bring *toys!*"

Simone lived for many years in Amsterdam with Cheryl. I could only send gifts by mail. When she came back, she still loved to read. Now it was fantasy books. We'd choose some in the store and talk about them for a long time. In ways like this I came to know her again.

Now we talk on the phone. I send gifts. I see them on holidays. I know that I have a place in their sense of family. But being a long-distance grandmother isn't optimal, and my aging hasn't helped.

Even here in Boulder my life with my grandchildren changed. Emma always loved to read. When she was small, we went to the library together. I showed her the fun of trolling through the stacks: how to pick out a book that might be interesting from looking at the cover or jacket description or opening page. This is a skill and a pleasure that I've honed since my own childhood, one spent immersed in libraries. I wanted to share it with her. Afterward, we'd have a snack together at the library café and chat. But then her mother started taking her to the bookstore—so much easier, I suppose. Then, with the advent of her own busy after-school life to add to this other means of procuring books, the charm of the library disappeared, and the library outings stopped. After she became a teenager, I had nothing to do with her reading life. Why should I?

Eliza and I share a love: ballet. I took her to movement class when she was four. Soon after, when she was old enough for ballet lessons, I was still the one who drove her and stayed to watch. I saw her energy and precise movement, and I found it fascinating to watch her begin to learn the steps that I knew so well. I would pick her up at school, bring her home for a snack, and wind her long hair into a bun for class. Only I did it just right, she'd say.

But when she was eight, she no longer wanted me as her ballet pal. "You are always *looking* at me, Grammy," she complained. She claimed ballet as her own and went on to advance from level to level. From then on, I was permitted to watch from the audience only.

However, over time I became less and less relevant to the girls. I tried to think of ways to stay a part of their lives. I began taking one or the other out for a treat, to buy books or have lunch or tea. We always had fun, but it often seemed that they were making time to do this for *me*. So as the years passed, I started to wait for an obvious reason to be together to arise. I gave Emma a shopping spree for her birthday a couple of years ago. It was a treat to watch her happily model "garments" at Nordstrom. I got to help Simone create a board game, a school assignment, in California. I've gone to different tea shops in Pasadena with Gabe—he loves tea—and I've enjoyed preparing it with him in his kitchen. I found a British series of ballet books for Eliza and introduced her to the great choreographer and impresario George Balanchine with a well-known DVD, *Dancing for Mr. B.*, featuring several of his ballerinas.

I would worry: Is this enough? Could I do better? Are my daughters disappointed? It is very hard to escape from the cookie baking lady, but I needed to see that our lives had developed in ways that were much more complicated than the cultural stereotype of grandmother permits.

Today my grandmother role is pretty fixed. In Boulder I am here, but I don't participate in much of the teenagers' daily life. Birthdays, performances, holidays. I follow their many activities primarily via conversations with their mothers; they are after all my daughters' favorite topic. I throw in commentary or advice along the way. I know that as I have aged, living with my arthritis, I am less easy to have around. I have trouble sitting in many chairs; don't engage in most sports any more.

What do I give my grandchildren? When I look at the stories that I have told, I see something that I hadn't ever really understood. As much as my tales are about tuning in to their favorite pastimes, they are also about what I have wanted to pass on to them: my passions and skills—reading; ballet. I still have these to offer. They are essential aspects of what makes me Grammy.

When Eliza performs, the family can see how good she is and how special. Yes, but I am the one who really knows what she does and how she does it. When I comment on a performance, I am specific about steps and positions in my praise. "I really liked your piqué turns." "Your arabesque is getting higher."

When Emma was doing her college applications, like her mother and aunts before her, she asked me to help with her essay. I was so happy that she understood and appreciated the grammar points that I couldn't help but make, along with some much more complex issues about the essay's governing ideas. She not only got it—she had fun!

I helped Simone, too, with her application essay to the Oakland School for the Arts High School. Her art is unique; I love her digital work. She was admitted, I'm happy to say.

What I give to Gabe is my appreciation. He is passionate about a magic card game that can be played in tournaments. When I am in California, I take him to the game store to learn about and buy the magic cards. His math skills are amazing to me. A couple of years ago, he told his mother how he was told to solve an equation in math class. He thought that the answer took too long to write out, so he came up with another, shorter way—one that was absolutely correct. "Wow," I said.

Now the kids are in their late teens. Emma with her fierce energy and beautiful mind attends Harvard College, where she develops her love for biology, new to her after her lifelong passion for musical theatre. (She still performs in student productions there, too.) Simone will attend Cooper Union School of Art. Her quirky and wonderful art, like her quirky and wonderful self, has blossomed. Eliza is studying to be a ballet dancer at the Houston Ballet, for dance is where her lovely spirit finds its physical form. Gabe has been admitted with early admission to Stephens Polytechnics Institute, where both his computer skills and art skills will be nurtured.

Our extended family always gathers at my house on for Christmas. These days, there is a brunch and then presents. Every year I struggle to find the perfect tree, always different. But by the time it is enveloped in the ornaments and lights and silver tinsel, the family's comment when they see it, year after year, is "It looks just the same! It looks like *your* tree!"

When grandchildren arrived in the family, at first that just meant many more presents and a lot of mess with wrapping paper. But as they grew, traditions developed just for them. My favorite is the tree trimming ritual, which started when they grew old enough to put the ornaments on the tree: old enough at least to try to put the tinsel on carefully and not in clumps. Later on they were old enough to listen to our stories—Branny's and mine—about each ornament's history. Today Emma and Eliza know those stories by heart, and each girl has her favorites and wants to put those particular ones on the tree.

Everybody likes the final moment: when I place on the top of the tree the angel that I made when I was ten! She has a red construction cone for her body. Her wings are made of wrapping paper with a pattern of cherries on a pale gold background, backed with thin cardboard, and they spread out to the side. At the top is a circle of ribbon, and right in the center is a hand-drawn cut-out face of a little girl: a smiley kid with pigtails, wearing a woolen cap with a pompom. She's me: *I* am the Christmas angel. Snap, goes the camera, and I am recorded for one more year. So many years.

I think that this and the other traditions that evolved especially for them, like a sleepover and dinner on Christmas Eve (always the same food, even the Sara Lee chocolate cake), may have meaning for them today *because* they are a part of their pasts. Simple pleasures, but they make me hope that the things that we used to do together form part of the way in which these young people understand themselves and their childhoods.

Still I miss the days when I was a truly needed grandmother. I was so much more central to their family life. But I know that these are different times, for me as well as for them and for their parents.

Recently, at a family party for Emma's high school graduation, I overheard her telling her aunt about her favorite English teacher. "One day she came into class," laughed Emma, "wearing a big hat and a cape! She tossed it around, spread her arms wide, and started to recite a poem. She's just like Grammy!"

That brief moment warmed my heart. It made me think that the Grammy whom she knows today is not just an oldish lady who has trouble sitting in folding chairs and couldn't come to all of her choir performances, but the Grammy whom she has known all of her life. I don't do the same things for or with my grandchildren that I used to do, but I am here, loving them always. My hope is that they love me in whatever way that makes sense now. As for me, my love for them is strong and abiding, a large component of who I am. I am a grandmother.

PART III

Love Forever True

8

True Love: The Search Begins

Family love has orchestrated my life, but another form of love has played an essential role for me, as well: romantic love. Love, romance, sex: a feeling, a goal, a joy, a disturbance, and even a punishment. For most of my life, I searched for romance and sought to keep it when it came my way. But if you're a devotee of romance, as I have been, and you're always searching for true love, lasting love, you get into trouble. How was I to know that they were not the same? How did I negotiate my joy in the thrills of romantic ardor with my abiding need to be safe and cherished? Not well, is the answer. I grew up thinking that waltzing down a moonlit street and "socks," as I called it (I meant home life, daily life), were part of the same package. I thought that if two people were soul mates, then they belonged together forever, and what led up to the "together forever" part was the romance. In this way, I conflated the terms "romance," "true love," and "forever after." Why should I not? As a girl, I learned from my culture that they were a package deal.

I also learned something else, very early and without knowing it: that the deeper you loved someone and the harder you tried to have this love returned, the more possible, even likely, it was that the person would turn away.

My emotional and psychological struggles with each of my parents were not understood by anyone involved, so they occupied a submerged place deep inside of me, but the goal for girls to achieve love and romance was writ large across the collective consciousness of modern American culture, and it was supremely powerful in the 1950s in my small New England city. I read all those novels. I listened to all those songs. I saw all those movies. School and theatre and dance class mattered a great deal, to be sure. But when I was a girl, romance was the designated goal. I ached for it. My mother had led me to believe early on that smart girls who weren't very pretty would have trouble in the romance game, but I still had my hopes. I don't know what the popular girls may have dreamed of, beyond the dresses, the dates, the kisses (my mother had been, and still was, a popular girl), but what I most wanted to get from it was a soul mate: someone who not only loved me but liked me, who not only liked me but was like me. We would understand one another completely and find fulfillment in that understanding.

(Actually, I did have a soul mate for a long time when I was young, my friend Chickie from Hillsboro Camp, but I saw her only nine weeks of the year, although we exchanged long and frequent letters over the remaining months. Of course I had no idea, living in a middle-class Jewish neighborhood in Providence, Rhode Island, in the 1950s, that girls counted.)

How did I imagine romance? To begin with, I wanted to be chosen—some enchanted evening, across a crowded room. Girls did not call boys on the phone; girls did not ask boys to dance.

Girls had to be *chosen*. And a girl with a big mouth and freckles, who happened to get straight As, was not the obvious choice. I learned this as a young teenager at those mortifying dances where I stood in a group of girls, all of us in our full skirts with petticoats beneath, Capezio flats, hair in ponytails, pretending that we were having a conversation with one another, all the while waiting for a boy to ask one of us to dance. When some boys ambled awkwardly across the room, girls did get asked, but never me. My crushes on boys in school were not only unreciprocated but also probably not even noticed. Still, I could always find romance in books.

Later, I used to teach courses on women and romance fiction at my university, for I studied the topic under an intellectual microscope, even as it wreaked havoc with my life. I would talk to my students about the "balloon lover," who exists for a time in a blown-up fantasy space, but ultimately the balloon deflates, I told them, and the lover turns out to be just a person. My head knew this, but my heart was another story. Once, after my divorce from my husband whom I had believed for many years was my true love, a new lover said to me, "Oh, Suzanne, you are looking for the Sunset Man (the one with whom you go off into the sunset), and he doesn't exist." This man walked off into his own sunset but without me.

Today I am a woman who has been married three times, and I have had other romantic relationships, as well. All in service of true love. Now, finally, I know that romantic love comes with the proviso that it will *not* stay. Possibly it may morph into other kinds of love, but often it will end dramatically, leaving scars that can last a lifetime.

But there were always books. As a young teenager, my favorite was an English novel called *Tryst*, by Elswyth Thane, written in the late 1930s. In *Tryst* Sabrina, an awkward, lonely young woman in her late teens, finds an empty study in a house rented by her family, a room full of wonderful books. She learns that the room belongs to a son of the family that owns the house. He is Hilary, a man in his early thirties, a CID officer who, upon being killed in the war, returns as a ghost to his room and finds Sabrina there. He makes his presence known to her by leaving books open at relevant pages, and they fall in love. The book's happy ending is that she dies in a car crash, as her parents are taking her away from the house and from what they see as her peculiar obsession with the room. Now she can join him forever in the room. No matter that he is a ghost. They have found one another, and true love cannot be thwarted. I was all for ghost lovers, especially when they loved books.

Indeed, it was very important to me that many of my favorite protagonists, reading girls like Sabrina in this more obscure novel but also the more famous Jo March, Anne Shirley, and of course Jane Eyre, got their man in one fashion or another, although some of the solutions created by their authors were rather contorted. Think about poor crippled Mr. Rochester or that most motherly lover, Mr. Bhaer. But romance for reading girls isn't so easy, as anyone who has lived it knows.

In the movies, I couldn't identify with a heroine like Doris Day, pretty and blond and perky (and a lot like my mother), but there was Audrey Hepburn, who may have been lovely but whose characters were always shy and awkward girls who stumbled into marvelous romances with wonderful heroes, like Gregory Peck. In *Roman Holiday* their romance brings out her strength of character and adventurous spirit. He is both sophisticated and gentle as well as handsome. A little like Phil, a.k.a. Greg Hecht.

My favorite play was *Private Lives*, by Noël Coward, a British classic from the 1930s, which is a tribute to the viability of true love. But in that play, true love—and the lovers—is terribly clever as well as romantic. (And sexy.) In fact, it is their recognition that they are both such social critics, such clever cynics, that makes one see that they belong together. In Coward's work, romance can and must go hand in hand with biting wit. Chickie was with me when I discovered the original cast recording in Sam Goody's, during my one and only visit to her in New York City. She shared my passion for "Dear Noël," as we called him to ourselves.

In *Private Lives* Amanda and Eliot meet after their recent divorce, when they are on separate honeymoons with new partners. They soon realize that they are still madly in love. So they run away together to their Paris apartment, love and quarrel intensely and cleverly, and finally run away together again—leaving their two new partners, conventional, dull people, to have their own dull, conventional romance. Thus true love, their kind of true love, reigns.

Even then, what I liked best was romance laced with wit, a tradition equally alive in Shakespeare's comedies like *Much Ado About Nothing*. I thrilled to love that was playful as well as passionate, where *smart girls* had their say. Thane's *Tryst* was another matter. No comedy there, but not only was the lovers' shared love of books the source and conduit of the romance, but the idea of true love conquering all, even death, was dead, as it were, center. "Once you have found her [or him], never let her go," as the French plantation owner sings in *South Pacific*.

Of course there are many sad stories bemoaning lost love, and I wouldn't even read *Anna Karenina* and *Madame Bovary* because I knew how they ended. But mostly, there was plenty of material wherever you turned to stir the hopes and fill out the plots that I desired. In novels like *Pride and Prejudice,* you had to get through the part where they hated one another, but that was always a clue, really, to show that they were meant to be together and that true love would conquer in the end. Of course, *Pride and Prejudice,* that ur-romance, has the cleverest heroine in English fiction.

Many years later, I wrote a book called *Reading From the Heart: Women, Literature, and the Search for True Love* (1994), in which I proposed that in certain plots not only were heroines who were badly mothered searching for another mother in their true love soul mate, the hero, but that the author (as a presence in the prose) could mother the reader during the reading process. I mention this because my goals for a beloved who would recognize my true self, formed in my youngest years, remained persistent, whatever I might have experienced along life's journey.

As a girl I hoped, and I waited. One thing I knew: true love, although inevitable, was not in my control: "I took one look at you / that's all I had to do / And then my heart stood still," said the song, but the "you" had to appear. Finally in my midteens, I actually dated three people. The first was a senior in my high school when I was a sophomore. It was a conventional double date, arranged by a girl whom I knew. We went to the movies and sat in the balcony, and he held my hand. He was cute, but nothing happened inside me. Kenny was dull and conventional. We started dating, usually with the other couple, but even though he sent me a large Valentine, our time together was brief, because I wouldn't make out with him. I didn't love him, so it didn't seem right. He stopped calling.

The next two were older. They were young men really. I met them in the theatre groups to which I belonged. One was a college student at the Rhode Island School of Design; the other, in his late twenties, was a journalist in the navy, stationed in Newport. With these young men, I went to a college party at someone's apartment; I even went to Boston to see a show. But the results were the same. No fooling around meant no more phone calls. I couldn't do it. I didn't like it. It felt wrong. I was pleased by the fact of them, that they would ask me out. But I didn't love them. And my sources had trained me too well to want anything less.

However, I didn't have too long to wait. I fell in love when I was fifteen, in 1957. That same year "Young Love" topped the charts: "They say for every boy and girl / there's just one love in this whole world / and I, I, I, I / found mine." True love was forever, so I married him when I was twenty-one. In between love and marriage was the romance.

Joseph Boris Bruno Bela Arnold Frederick Juhasz, Hungarian refugee, then Brown University Freshman and ex-high-school debate star, along with his friend Colston Chandler, appeared one afternoon at my high school to help us form a debate team.

There he was, sitting on the table in front of the classroom where interested students had assembled, legs swinging as he spoke with his sexy accent, in crewneck sweater, khaki pants, and sneakers: bright slanty brown eyes, curly brown hair, and big ears. My heart gave a flop, but I saw no reason why he'd ever notice me, a little high-school girl. It was just a crush, I knew. But I did manage to get myself and my best friend Patti elected president and vice president of the newly formed Hope High School Debate Society. In this way, she and I came to be friends with Joe and Colston, our advisors, as the debate club met weekly.

That's how it happened that Joseph arranged for us to have a practice debate at Brown with their freshman team on the idiosyncratic topic, "This House Prefers 'Little Lulu' to 'Classic Comics.'" Patti and I joined Joseph and Colston for an evening. She and I were supporting Little Lulu, and they were on the side of Classic Comics. I practiced my arguments daily, often in the shower. I was terrified, but the event actually turned out to be fun. And Patti and I didn't do so badly, for brand-new debaters.

Afterward, the four of us celebrated at a college hangout on Thayer Street, and then it was time to go home. But, and this is where the magic began, Joseph asked if I could stay longer. Patti's father was to pick us up, but Joe said he'd take me home later in a taxi! He and I walked to the large living room of his dorm. And then we talked and talked, until it grew later yet. Finally he called the cab, but when we arrived at my house, he got out with me and said he'd walk back to Brown, about two miles.

What were we talking about? Everything, of course. Baring our souls, as we were meant to do. For hours into the long, long night on the couch in my living room, until sometime near dawn, we kissed. I had no problem with that. Slowly he took out the bobby pins from my hair in its tight French twist so that it fell to my shoulders, and then, more slowly yet, he unzipped the back of my gray dress. I delighted in every minute of this, for I had fallen in love. He didn't do any more: just held me and kissed me for a very long time. When it was dawn, he started off on his long walk back to Brown.

Our conversation had instilled in both of us the thrill of finding that long cherished goal: a soul mate. Clearly, despite all of our differences—he was Hungarian, I was American; he was Catholic, I was Jewish; he was a college man, I was a high-school student—we belonged together. He was smart and thoughtful and clever.

We both had ideas about everything in the world. A boy who had escaped the Communist regime at twelve, who was four years older than I was, he nonetheless took my ideas seriously. I found his ideas fascinating. I suppose that I was playing Audrey Hepburn to his Gregory Peck. Or better yet, Samantha from *Tryst* to his Hilary. (Amanda and Elyot were beyond us. We were *not* sophisticated!)

Gypsy violinists and Tokay in a tiny Hungarian nightclub on New York's East Side. Waltzing all by ourselves at the fraternity Christmas dance, for no one else knew how, with applause for us at the end. (Joseph couldn't dance when I met him, but now he's first on the dance floor.) We won a prize: three tiny china bears. Soo romantic.

Since he was a fraternity man, we were "pinned" in my senior year of high school and engaged when I was in college. We designed our engagement ring ourselves at a tiny shop in Greenwich Village. The ring was a flower: gold petals with the tiniest of diamonds at the center, surrounded by six small cabochon sapphires. Alex has it now.

In high school Joseph had starred as a debater and had received a debate scholarship to Brown University. But because he was a proud young man and saw that as taking charity, he chose instead to attend Brown on a navy scholarship, which meant that he would repay the four years as a naval officer.

He was my true love. It had happened. My parents didn't quite agree. He was Catholic, and I actually started attending mass with him because I wanted to share in his life, especially what mattered most to him. Early in our relationship, my parents banned him from our house and me from a church. So I would see him at Brown and not tell them, although I did stop going to mass. I felt strange there, anyway. Finally, they allowed him back, and we continued as before. In many ways my parents were actually quite pleased with him. He was smart and hand-some, he had a wonderful accent, and he was very charming. His European identity was a plus: exotic, different. He didn't believe in Valentine's Day, true, because they didn't have such a thing in Hungary, but they did have Viennese waltzes.

Thus Suzy and Joe continued on their romantic journey until I graduated from college, and I was perfectly satisfied. I loved the kissing and the cuddling, but no, I did not lust for him. It was the 1950s, and no one, certainly not me, expected me to lust. I was saving myself for my wedding night, with my beautiful gown and peignoir set, when everything about sex would be revealed, and that seemed perfectly appropriate to me. When we stayed at the romantic old Fifth Avenue Hotel in New York, as we did several times for special occasions, I insisted on separate rooms.

I look back and wonder how I got away with it. But my behavior and my morality were not entirely out of place when I was a young woman. We did as much as I was willing to do, but we never went "all the way." Even at Bennington, where the girls prided themselves on having sex lives and being very open about it, I did not participate in their ideas. *My* romance was like the ones in the novels: all about passionate emotion, without mention of what happened later.

Later would be the culmination, I knew, of our romance. Six years after we met we were married, and then it came, the start of our honeymoon. Sex at last. But the earth did not turn nor the skies blaze, as I expected. We kissed, and there was his moving penis inside me; we kissed again. But were married—and we were so happy that the skies didn't seem all that important, after all.

Joseph and I had a beautiful family and a long marriage. Life was full to bursting: children, careers—not so simple for either of us, but so very worth it. Berkeley, back to Bennington, Lewisburg, Santa Cruz, and finally Boulder, as we tried to secure a job for me, too. Even Dunedin, New Zealand, where Joseph took a visiting position with a famous psychologist, and I found myself teaching assistant to the Dean of Arts, the formidable Margaret Dalziel.

Why, then, did we divorce after seventeen years of marriage and a twenty-four year relationship? The reasons are never possible to explain adequately because of the layers upon layers of complexity in our relationship, but not surprisingly they had to do with work and sex. Work, because although we both had PhDs from Berkeley, he could get real jobs and I couldn't.

Ironically, after five years I finally got my own assistant professorship in Colorado, and he most generously followed me there. But then the psychology department at CU would not hire *him* because I had a job in the same college. He went from instructorship to instructorship at other institutions, even as I had done, for five years before he recreated himself as an environmental psychologist and thus found an appointment in the UC Boulder College of Environmental Design. During all this time I did not sympathize all that much with his plight. I now fault myself for this, but then it seemed, well, that I had gone through it, and now it was his turn. It didn't really occur to me that he was only in this plight because of his goodness to me. Or maybe it did, and the idea of his *goodness to me* rankled. The truth was that we were both victims of the rampant sexism that prevailed always and everywhere, which had nothing to do with either of us personally. Sexism because no one would hire me as a faculty wife, sexism because a man had to help me so that I could properly enter the profession for which I was so highly qualified.

For sexism there was, even in our own relationship, despite his wonderful qualities. Joseph was a Hungarian male, and he had met me when I was really a child. Whether it was helping me with my class papers or keeping the checkbook, he took charge. He made the decisions, and I generally acquiesced. When my professional friends came to visit, especially those who were not local, they noted our hospitality and my subservience. I didn't get it, because I was so used to it. Only after I became a feminist, fifteen years into our relationship, did stirrings of doubt or twinges of anger occur.

It wasn't just jobs: it was sex, too. All through the late 1960s and 1970s, free love was in. Even feminists got on this bandwagon, eventually, claiming that women had the right to own their bodies. He had an affair; finally, I had one, too. But no matter what we were supposed to feel, the truth was that we both felt utterly betrayed by the other. He had girlfriends whom he didn't love, he said. Eventually, I tried, too. But I was always looking for love (in all the wrong places); inevitably, I would be rejected by these men.

On a cold winter's day in 1980, with icy rain streaming down the windows, Joseph and I sat in our living room, and between us was the word "divorce." I was the one who said it. I am sure that Joseph would never have done so, and he would have gone on as we were. However, our love had become strained to the breaking point, as I understood it, and I wanted to try again. But how could I, how could we, hurt the children and our beautiful family? Our commitment to them and the love that we shared for them was profound. But I was so angry at him, and I believed that the anger had finally erased the long love between us. I hated my need for something that I thought we had lost; I hated my lies; I wanted a life that was clean again. What else was there to do?

That day Joseph cried. A man who never cried. During our conversation, he said that I was doing this now because I had just been granted tenure and promotion and could afford not to have his care. He himself, who had had to start all over at CU, in a new college, a new kind of psychology, was not nearly so professionally stable. He had done this for me, I knew, of course I knew, but I believed that his new field, environmental psychology, pleased and suited him. Furthermore, I didn't see the connection, but it was probably there, beneath this and all the sexual brouhaha. I remained adamant, for I thought that I was doing the right thing.

Definitely joint custody, we agreed, which took many forms over the years. But to begin with, a separation to see how that went. However, he soon decided to marry his present girlfriend, so quickly there was divorce. Our twenty-seven years together was over.

It turned out that finding someone new was a lot harder than having an affair. I was really available now—smart, successful, and on my own: a frightening combination. I soon found out as well that my hard-won "freedom" was laced with difficulty. I hated sharing the children. I was ill-equipped to run my own finances, fix things around the house, or know what was wrong with my car. Most significantly, I, who had never lived alone, had to meet that ogre "Loneliness" head-on. I wasn't very good at that, either. But I was back on the trail, searching for true love. I knew that it had to be out there.

In fact, I had already experienced it a second time, but in the years when my marriage was unraveling. I wore a hat with yellow ribbons streaming down the back, while my lover wore a straw boater and paddled a canoe down a blue river. Romance!

I once wrote a short story called "The Romantic Adventuress." When I sent it to *Redbook Magazine*, they rejected it with the comment that while it was well written, it was too over the top to be realistic. In fact, it was sheer autobiography, every bit. It described my great adulterous romance of the 1970s, particularly special because Reginald (the fictitious name that I gave to my lover) offered the combination of romance, cleverness, and humor that had always drawn me to those witty lovers of fiction. Reginald, as handsome as Gregory Peck, had the flair for repartee that so excited me. This is why we had names for the characters whom we acted out in our little adventures together. Mine was Benita, but he called me B, and I called him R. I wore that hat, and he wore his straw boater, when we staged our outing on the river (well, it was a pond, and the punt was a rowboat). The requisite champagne and strawberries were aboard. However, the boat had a leak and started to sink, so we had to grab our props and trudge unromantically through the muck to the shore, laughing all the while at the silliness of it all. We waltzed in the streets and picnicked on oysters, and we made love in the most incongruous of places—mountainsides and even snowbanks, often during the most inclement of weathers, for we were young and agile. We kept up our banter and laughter through it all, for that was the point: we were playing out our romantic fantasies. We were Amanda and Elyot.

But we were not playing, of course, not entirely. We were in love. And he didn't like that part. It scared him. Consequently, he would end the affair, over and over again. Each time this happened, I would suffer and grieve. Then we'd meet on the path, and our feelings would flare up, and we'd start all over again. Once a waitress said, "Whatever that thing is that you have, you should share it around." That thing was real enough, but we were illicit, even though it was the 1970s, when "open marriage" was in style. He was not telling his wife, and his guilt or fear or whatever it was would finally cause the next rupture. Yet I wanted the socks. Dirty socks in the hamper of our home. I thought that the two elements came together to create a rich, fully realized existence. I thought that my life depended upon this. "No socks," he said.

He was not brave: I was. He loved that about me: my imagination, my daring, and perhaps even my persistence. He told me so. I led him to places where he wanted to go but would never have done so without me. Up to a point, however, only up to a point. For him, romance was one thing, but marriage was another.

Whenever we were apart, our romance became the stuff of my poetry, for this was the only way that I knew to hang on to him and the world that we had created, with all of its icons: wildflowers and shells and even begonias, for he had given this plant as a gift. I shared these poems with my women's writing group. I also blatantly read them at poetry readings and even published some. There's a little chapbook, published in 1978, containing a long poem that I wrote about one of R's "journeys," which is what we called our time apart.

Today all this public testimony embarrasses me. What was I thinking? In my defense I have to say that it was not only the 1970s; it was the feminist 1970s. Our job as feminists as we saw it was to tell the truth of women's lives, hidden for so long. "Women's poetry" was a concept that had never existed before we created it, and I was a woman poet. I told the "truth" about my life in my consciousness-raising group and on the printed page, for I had the skill to put it there. My reward as a feminist was to have someone come up to me after a reading and say, "Me, too. Thank you for saying it."

But that wasn't my greatest reward. As a writer, I was able to give shape and form and a continued existence to my experience, for I believed that my words could do that. I wove tales of my affair because I couldn't hang on to it, and it was feeding me: the excitement, the thrill, and the passion, even as I saw them as routes to an end. I still believed that high romance was the sign of true love and that in the arms of true love the self would grow and flourish. My marriage had run aground; my present culture gave me permission to stray, so I did. I wasn't looking for sexual adventure, really, but for love, what my husband and I seemed to have lost along the way.

My husband knew about this relationship: he officially sanctioned it. I know, however, that he was angry; I was angry, too, about his relationships. But we persisted. I don't know what his reasons were, but mine I have explained. Why do I understand only now something much deeper about R: that he was so like my father—in his charm, his handsomeness, and his weakness? Even as my delightful father fled from me when I asked for more honesty and more overt love, so R did the same. My father told me not to struggle with life so much, to take it as it came. R told me that I was the stuff of his fantasies, but that ultimately, fantasies were not real, and he would not disturb the life that he had made.

In his way, R was like my mother, too, wanting parts of me only and dismissing others. I learned from her that my imagination, my skills, and my successes were what made me appealing, but my deeper and even darker parts, my vulnerabilities, weaknesses, and fears, did not exist for her. Where was she then? Gone. For R, something like this was equally true. But in his case, being gone was literal, whereas for her, it was purely psychological. Still, each time that I used my gifts, including my charm to attract, and then tried to offer the rest of me, that old demon, rejection, reasserted itself. But how could I stop trying? I want true love: here, here are *my* dirty socks!

I chose my second husband, Bill Reinhardt, because he appeared to be unlike anyone to whom I'd ever been attracted. He was not, as he put it once, speaking from his Oklahoman background, a "high-stepper." But he wanted me. I thought I that I would try an experiment, since the high-steppers never stayed in the end. He was gentler, less outgoing, less, "masculine," shall we say. He was brilliant, but he had no gift with words. Nor did he have sophistication or charm. He was a logician, and he lived for many hours of each day somewhere high in his mind, where his thought processes were slow, careful, and meticulous. When he sat at the dinner table with me and my daughters, he had difficulty following the rapid conversation; he didn't get the jokes as they flew past. Soft spoken, kind, and good, he was a lovely man, but he was not energetic, not dashing, and not, I thought, someone like me.

I first met him because we were both on a university committee. I sat in rooms with him and occasionally thought, "What an unappealing man." He had a scraggly little beard at which he often picked, and he wore polyester pants. He contributed little to the committee deliberations. And that was that—until I met him one day on the path at the university and stopped to say hello, simply because we knew one another. I was on sabbatical that year, only just divorced and living alone in the little house that I'd bought, seeing my girls for half of every week: alternating weekdays or weekend, but no longer really *living* with them. We struck up a conversation, and it turned out that he was recently separated from the wife of his long marriage, and he was lonely, too. It was a good conversation, I remember—longer than I'd meant it to be—for he was thoughtful and sensitive, despite the little beard.

When he asked me for a date, I did not refuse. Our date was, I must admit, a little peculiar. He said, laughing, that I could have my choice between eating at a good restaurant or sharing a bottle of very fine wine over dinner at his home. I chose the latter, as I was meant to do, and the dinner itself turned out to be bread, cold cuts, and cheese, which we ate on his kitchen table, because the dining room table was covered with papers and journals. Odd, to say the least, but the wine was amazing, and he was very sweet. We talked and talked, as his teenaged kids, a boy and a girl, came in and out. Odd indeed, but it was enough to begin a romance.

Long phone conversations became the norm, as shared interests and ideas flourished. And the sex, when it finally happened, was lovely. As in all things, he was considerate, sweet, and surprisingly accomplished.

I fell in love slowly, because he was not my "type," and he was indeed rather strange, a man living in a chaotic everyday world that he could not control. His was a big house, and it had not been cleaned or ordered in months. He built piles of papers and objects, and once built, they never moved. I questioned his ability to function in the world, only on the long yellow sheets of paper, where he endlessly scribbled what I knew to be equations of some sort.

Then I thought a new thought. "Maybe he is exactly the kind of person I need: someone who will not compete with but cherish me, someone so otherworldly that he will not find my ambition and accomplishments threatening after a while. Someone in many ways more like a girl than a guy." As the weeks passed, and his eagerness, gentleness, and insight expanded, I thought more and more that I had stumbled into something rather remarkable. When upon my instigation he shaved the beard, bought some new clothes, and most importantly, began to glow with happiness, I saw that he was indeed a handsome man.

And so we became an unlikely couple. As I entered into the new terrain of the mathematics department, I learned that people like him, nonverbal men who could not make conversation at parties, were the norm, not the exception. I learned as well that what he was scribbling on those yellow pads was significant scholarship, even ground-breaking, albeit I could not understand it at all. He could understand *my* work, however, and indeed, he was an admirable critic of it.

Life with me, so different from what I learned had been the peculiarity of his marriage, helped to lessen his awkwardness, build his confidence in himself, and even reveal his latent grace. True, I could not share many of his interests, although in the early days I certainly tried. For example, he was a Quaker, and at first I attended meetings, but I could not be comfortable there. Nor did I fare well with his children, who were difficult for me to understand.

But privately we created a life together that was precious, profound, and often joyful. Early in our relationship I had told him the story of a half-remembered moment in my childhood, when I woke on my birthday to discover a doll that I had wanted sitting on my dresser. Just there. The thrill of that unexpected delight had stayed with me throughout the years. Telling this was just a moment in a long conversation, but on the morning of my first birthday with him, a brightly colored stuffed clown doll was on my dresser. He'd tried to meet this half-understood need in me. "Clown," we called the doll, and I have him to this day. For Bill was indeed a romantic man, and my jewelry box now holds the antique earrings, necklaces, and even watches that he would give to me on special occasions, because he knew that I loved them. Quite simply, he adored me.

To be so cherished was a gift that I wanted more than any-thing. I loved him—for that and for his profound goodness as a human being. But I refused to *marry* him. My own feelings for him were more ambivalent than his for me. I knew that I was not with a person who was my idea of a lifelong partner. We were so different, and he was so odd, so troubled. But after a few years I agreed to buy a house together, inching toward the future that he envisioned. Still, I did not trust our situation. In addition, I was divorced from the man whom I had considered my true love, never imagining that such a love could fail us both. That divorce still shamed me, as much as I believed and still do that it was right.

Finally, however, after a couple of years, I decided that mar-riage would be a good idea after all, that taking the step would squash my doubts and help me to commit to our life and to the love that we truly shared. In our married life, we had to weather his depression. His new work was progressing very, very slowly. He knew and I learned that early success such as he had experienced followed by difficulty in later years was common in his field, but that didn't make things any easier for him. He was experiencing problems with his teenage children. His withdrawn son was becoming more and more interested in guns and swords and martial arts, and Bill was a pacifist. His daughter was a sweet girl, but she wanted me to be a mother to her, and I didn't feel able to do this. He felt enormous stress from his drawn-out divorce—and probably from whatever else was gnawing at him, which may well have had to do with me, for all I knew. But he was clearly suffering, and I was, too, as I watched him day after day sit at the breakfast table in his pajamas, working on his equations, growing more and more remote. The piles, as I called them, continued to grow. I would relegate them to his basement office, but they would never diminish, and slowly they would climb the steps back toward the house. They made me crazy, symbols of all about him that distressed me so deeply.

Yet there was much good as well, and I tried to put my concentration there. I was committed now, and that was that. I could put my history of unrequited love behind me; even, perhaps, my sad, unfulfilled love affairs with my parents, for here was a man who would never go away and never turn his gaze from mine. This is what I had been craving forever. Joseph was like that, too, and therefore a "sunset man," as well: but the price that he demanded—obedience—was too high, or so it seemed.

But then, eight years into my relationship with Bill, I had a life-altering discovery or made a life-altering decision, however one wants to see it: I decided that I was a lesbian. I fell madly in love again, but this time it was with a woman, and all those old long-buried feelings of romantic passion flared up again with a vengeance.

9

The Search Continues

What a cliché: I fell in love with my therapist. She wasn't my first therapist, and I'd had special feelings for the others before her. But I'd never experienced full-blown erotic transference, the term for what happened to me this time, as it has done to many other patients before me. But this is my story, and my experience was huge. And, oh yes, she was a lesbian.

For years I felt all of the many stages of passionate love for her: joy, longing, hope, frustration, pain. I knew them all. My intense emotions epitomized the romantic passion that I had wanted all of my life, along with the unhappiness that seems to go with it. Why not, when this kind of therapy so often reawakens the patient's earliest emotional situation: usually with a parent, frequently with a mother. Because my desires occurred this time in the "safe space" of therapy, I allowed myself to feel them to the fullest, in the ways that I always wanted to do. And because I was in therapy and not in "real life," my therapist and I would explore these feelings together. This process itself is believed to create an understanding of the patient's unresolved issues and, as a consequence, lead to development and change.

I understand all of this. I understood it from the start, for I had spent a long time in my forties studying on my own various schools of psychoanalysis, especially object relations, if only because much of it spoke to my personal concerns. Consequently, I was interested in the process itself as well as what happened to me in it. Initially, this was what provoked my excitement in this particular experience. But then along came the transference— boom. It turns out that it's one thing to know about it and quite another to feel it. Feeling it is falling in love, pure and simple.

I started to see her in in the early '90s. She was recommended to me "because she was so smart." And indeed she was: from the start she asked me difficult and unexpected questions. She made me *think*, and I liked that. She had a wicked sense of humor, as well. I warmed to her right away. I also liked the kind of psycho-analytical-based therapy that she practiced. It was challenging and profound, and it created an intimate therapeutic relation-ship different from any that I had encountered before, with its close attention to every nuanced emotion, the importance given to the interchange between therapist and client.

I have always been turned on, as it were, by intelligence. Now there was hers and mine in tandem, an interchange that never ceased to excite me. There was the room, set apart from the rest of my life. There was the relationship, developing such intimacy by means of the intense interaction and also because evading the truth, even social propriety, was not allowed. The questions had to be answered truthfully, and often the truth was unexpected, forgotten, or never considered, revelatory in small and bigger ways. Her own truth, too, was real, in the way that she responded or probed. Back and forth, back and forth. Of course I was but one of many clients, and all received the same consideration. But this did not discount the fact that we shared something, something about her as well as about me, and the something was more profound than most of what I experienced in "real" life. I had been craving this as long as I could remember. In the quiet room, our relationship came into being.

Much of our conversations were devoted, in particular, to an exploration of my lifelong search for love and its companion experience, as I understood it, rejection. Very quickly I saw her as someone like a mother, as I sought from her all that I seem to have missed the first time around. And just as quickly, or perhaps it was the same thing, I began to love her.

Two things occurred that caused me to wonder if she might be a lesbian. Before my very first session, when I was sitting in the waiting room, I recognized a woman coming out of her office who I knew was a lesbian. That in itself meant nothing in particular. But then, one day soon afterward in the library parking lot I saw my therapist entering the building with another woman. They were holding hands. "Aha," I thought. This was fairly circumstantial evidence, I know, but I was intrigued. I thought that I would just ask her. At the next session I said, "Are you a lesbian?"

She answered, "Yes." And then, she asked as therapists do, "Why do you want to know?" We had to discuss this many, many times over the course of our eight years together.

I was heterosexual, but my discovery of her lesbianism strangely capitulated my feelings into a new place altogether. In the days that followed, whenever I thought about her, which was pretty much all of the time, I found myself experiencing the most intense feelings of physical desire! It was astonishing. Suddenly I was madly, passionately in love. I had been with Bill for eight years, and the early days of romance were long gone. But here I was again. The world was imbued with her presence, and I counted the hours till our next session.

It took me a while, however, to tell her any of this. I was embarrassed and ashamed. Later she would say, "I've experienced transference many times before, but never so suddenly. Do you know why this happened to you?" She'd say it many times, and many times I would try to answer.

Soon my feelings for her, for the room, for what occurred there, became the most important part of my life. All else around me paled. I continued to deal competently with the all-elses: my work at the university, my research and writing, and of course my family. My three daughters were young women now, each tugging at me to go her separate way. There was my patient if phlegmatic husband, along with a difficult ex-husband, as well as my aging parents, as always problematic for me.

But I was in the thrall of romantic passion with a vengeance: the longing, the ambiguous gratification. For the therapeutic relationship is at once real and not real, balancing delicately between the past and the present, the world of the room and the world outside it. All I knew was that those forty-five minutes mattered so much, and they were so short. Always so short. My suffering was as great as my joy.

I yearned to be back. I would sit in the waiting room, imagining the door opening, and there she would be. She would say, "Hello, Suzanne," but nothing further until we were settled in our places. We had to walk down a hall to get to her office, and the rule was "no conversation until the session starts." She was very strict; there were many rules. But then we could begin, and then she was kind and concerned, funny, sweet, wherever the conversation went that day. There was a large painting in the room—an abstract scene of trees being blown by a strong wind—and many special objects: a lovely shell, a green glass bowl, and a small wood carving of a bird; to me they were talismanic. It was a sacred place, the room. I could be an adult in the room, and often I was, but I was also an adolescent or a child. My feelings and expressions of love were hyperbolic; my craving for love could be total. I interacted with her on all of these levels. Always, I never wanted to leave the room, and I began to suffer as the time drew near. But it arrived, and that was absolutely that. We never went past that minute: there were rules. I would have to go, heart turning over.

Of course there was the cardinal rule of therapy: thou shalt not have sex with a patient. This could not happen, nor would it happen. Not once did I ever expect it. I wasn't even a lesbian, after all. But I dreamed about it, shocking as that was. However, it was always a fantasy, not a plan. I knew from the annals of therapy that this has occurred and more than once, with dire consequences for both patient and therapist, but I never wanted to hurt either of us in this way. What I wanted *to happen* was one thing only. I wanted her to say that she loved me. I really do think that I meant "love," not sex. I wanted her to love me. But those were words she never said, for these words are also against the rules.

I knew the rules, but nonetheless, the fact that she would not tell me what I needed to hear felt to me like rejection. Even the fact that I had to leave at the designated time, not a second afterward, seemed a rejection. My mind understood, but my heart did not. In this way I was indeed recapitulating my long romantic pattern, initiated with my earliest loved one, my mother. All of this was good fodder for analysis, but it didn't make the pain go away.

It seems that the lesbian part of the equation was what initially tipped me over. But I was heterosexual! I had gone through all those years of second-wave feminism, when so many women were either lesbians to begin with, proud to assert their identities at last in this new environment, or they were "becoming" lesbians to assert their feminism: to stop "sleeping with the enemy," as the phrase went. But I didn't do that, even though I was 100 percent feminist. I recognized the fact of male chauvinism: I saw that men—in organizations or personally—were responsible for women's second-rate, unnatural, and unjust social status. I fought for women's rights everywhere and especially in the academic world. But I was straight.

My most embarrassing straight story is about a moment when at a conference I went to a feminist party in one of the hotel rooms. There were a lot of lesbians there. A group of women were gathered around a photograph, and I looked, too. "Oh, isn't he handsome," I said, when I saw the person in the photo. They all laughed. I suddenly realized: "he" was a "she"! I fled. I couldn't even apologize for my faux pas, which would have made me seem more foolish yet, so far from a lesbian sensibility was I.

Nevertheless, in the '80s I did once try with a woman. She was an old friend, and she was bisexual. One night, over dinner at her house, she told me that she was in love with me and wanted to have sex. I admit to having been rather thrilled by her declaration. No woman had ever asked me before. Thus, after a brief flirtation, dancing around the idea for a couple of days, I came back for another dinner. Afterward, we did have sex. Tense as we both were, I rather liked it, I discovered, so for a day or so we thought of ourselves as "girlfriends." But much as I wanted to, I didn't really love her, and as always I needed that part. I kept making excuses not to do it again. And so the "affair" quietly died. Luckily, our friendship remained.

Yet years later, when I was in this new therapy, something turned inside me. I was fifty years old, and here I was, feeling lust and desire and all those urgent stirrings for the woman sitting across from me. Inside her office, I would struggle with these feelings and my attempts to express them to her—and to analyze them, naturally. In a while I stopped being embarrassed and became proud, even, albeit perennially frustrated. Outside of her office, I would walk down the street and look at women in a brand-new way.

Suddenly, my lifetime of intense friendships with girls and women took on a new meaning for me. Maybe I had been a lesbian all along, I thought, just unable to understand the kind of love that I experienced. What did I know about lesbians, anyway, until 1970? Until feminism, they certainly weren't visible in any culture in which I operated, not even at Bennington. Or maybe I never noticed. I'd read *The Well of Loneliness,* that lesbian bible, when I was a teenager, but I didn't like it because it had an unhappy ending; that's all I remembered. And what did I understand, really, about my less-than-successful sexuality in my marriages? It is true that I didn't like it all that much, but that was my embarrassing problem, or so I believed. Now I thought about my attraction to those girls and women in my past and wondered, "Was it sexual?" Maybe. Once this situation became known, inside the therapist's office it was necessary to analyze it. "Why do you love me?" "What are you feeling?"

The notebooks began. I was a dedicated journal writer, but during this period, I recorded *everything* that happened in *every* session—and soon I was going twice a week. Later she remarked that she had probably made a mistake in adding another session, that perhaps I wasn't ready to come so often, and that this had extenuated, not controlled, my intensity. I didn't see it that way. I saw it as more of her. Not as much as I wanted, surely, but more than I'd had before. The journals served to compensate in their particular way for the absences that I found so difficult. For me words kept the feeling going, extending the experiences themselves. When I read those journals now, I am both embarrassed and intrigued. Embarrassed by the sheer excess of my emotions and the repetition of my expression of them. Over and over and over. But that's how therapy (and obsession) works: over and over and over.

But I am also intrigued by the journals now because the entries demonstrate the therapeutic process at work: what she said, what I said, what she said, what I said. When reading, you can see the subtleties of the interaction. I see that I am not always histrionic. I am thoughtful in response to her measured calm. We move to difficult places. I learn. But always I yearn.

Words had another function in those journals: they gave me a place to say all of the things that I did not dare to say in the session, for I was frightened of her: always believing that if I said the wrong thing, she would send me away, tell me to leave, that it was over. Even when I got to the point where I could say even this to her and tell her how I suffered torment after leaving a session, having decided that I had said that crucial wrong thing that would cause my dismissal, still my anxiety would continue over the days until I made it back to the room, and the door was not locked to me, and we would go over the moment that I had found so critical, and she would show me how it was benign, after all. Even then, the next time around I would go through the same process all over again. "Why did I say that? Why didn't I know not to say that?" Pages and pages of words: my only defense against what I perceived as her power.

It must be underlined that this was transference, where by projecting on to the therapist the qualities of her mother (shall we say), the patient reexperiences that relationship: a drama and a narrative that she has known all of her life. I understood that the therapist's multiple task was both to allow these feelings to flower fully, so that they could be analyzed, and at the same time to offer the patient other kinds of responses to them, a different way to understand both the feelings and herself so that her life could actually change. Take my fear of rejection, which was always accompanied by a belief that I was responsible for it, simply by saying or doing the wrong thing. It was not rational, one might say, but again, it clearly recapitulated my relationship with my mother. And with others, especially Reginald. Usually the "wrong thing" was just loving too much. Was that really what I was feeling with Janet? I always remembered her turning away as being caused by some action of mine with which she did not agree. But when I discovered those old greeting cards and their outpouring of my girlish love, I wondered what had happened in the earliest days.

My belief in words had another dimension here. For my sheer pleasure in the therapeutic process itself, the intimacy created by the meeting of minds and the subtle interchange of ideas and questions and answers was an intimacy created with words. There was no acting on these feelings. In therapy, words are primarily what one has to develop a relationship. I was good at words, and so was she.

Of course we talked about lesbians. I wanted to convince her of the truth of my feelings. I wanted her, and I also wanted what she had: the magical world of the lesbians. I wanted to be a lesbian.

I had a few lesbian friends, and I started telling them my feelings about not only my therapist in particular but also women in general. They were encouraging, very. For one thing, they tried to give me access to the lesbian community in Boulder. I went to a party! The room was filled with women, and I didn't know any of them. I tried to meet and mingle. But I have to say that it wasn't easy. They were all younger than I was, no one was an academic (my friend was a librarian), and it seemed to put them off when I said that I was a professor. In fact, I didn't have much in common with most of the people with whom I tried to talk, so the conversations died. Still, they were lesbians, and to me that was terribly exciting in and of itself. I didn't know much about live lesbians, after all, only what I read in books. For at the time I was devouring lesbian novels, for the genre existed, I discovered: both pulp fiction and some that were better. Reading is always my favorite way to inhabit any world.

But I persevered. I went to a lesbian talent show in Denver and watched the women, some in full butch or femme regalia, parade around the auditorium. I learned what lesbians looked like in the 1990s, and I found that I was attracted to them all, both the butches and the femmes. I learned to recognize my attraction and to release it in myself, even if I never got to talk to any of them. As usual, they were too busy talking to one another. I even went to a Gay Pride March, which was loud and hot and not, I'm sorry to confess, a lot of fun. I was trying to be out, but who cared?

Then I joined the Faculty-Staff Gay and Lesbian organization on campus. At that time it was a social group, a place for primarily closeted people to get together. Later, the politics and even the academic possibilities emerged. This world was more familiar to me. Some people said at first, "Why are *you* here, Suzanne?" But they were welcoming to anyone who needed their friendship.

"Why are you doing this, Suzanne?" my therapist would ask. And I would answer that I wanted to be a lesbian. Or that I was a lesbian. Wasn't I, if I sexually desired one woman and now other women? Even if I wasn't having sex with any woman? I was in love with a woman. It was confusing.

I even started talking about my feelings to family and friends who were heterosexual. I talked about my therapy, because it was so exciting to me, and I talked about desiring women. I talked because my emotions were so big that the little room could not contain them, because to me they were extraordinary, and because I was a woman in love—with therapy, with my therapist, and with women. Generally, my confidante would say how nice and change the subject fast. I embarrassed everyone, I know, and today I embarrass myself just thinking about it. Cardinal rule number one: one does not talk to others about what happens in therapy. Therapy is private. And perhaps even more important, therapy isn't really interesting to anybody else but the client. Cardinal rule number two: people in love, obsessed by their feelings, the beloved's wonderfulness, are embarrassing and boring and *should not talk about it*. I knew all of this, but nothing could hold me back. For I felt that my love had changed me utterly: that as I discovered an awakened sexuality, my identity itself had altered in a primary way. Because it wasn't just sex: it was an idea that I had about relationships. With a woman, I thought, I might not be so threatening as I was to men, just because I was smart and accomplished. We might be able to talk more about our feelings, become more intimate. After all, my friendships with women had always been the backbone of my social world.

I had become a faux teenager. I would walk down the Boulder Mall and notice all the cute women in a new way. I wanted a girlfriend! I was on the lookout, and I took the first opportunity that came along. I met a woman at a campus GLB meeting. She was pretty, small, slender, with red gold hair, and we seemed to have a lot in common. She was a secretary on campus, and I was a professor, but what did status matter? We flirted; we met for tea at the Walrus Café, a gay meeting place, I discovered. We took long walks. We necked in her car. We even necked in her apartment. I thought, "Oh, wow!" But oddly, she would not have sex with me. She declared at the outset that we "had to wait a month," because of her own "issues." So we didn't go "all the way." Everything but. In the end, and it didn't take long, about a month, she declared it over. How embarrassing is that?

Where was my poor husband in all of this drama? Suffering, angry, helpless—caught in a plot that he'd never imagined. Now all of his problems, weaknesses, and irritating habits became fuel for my reasoning: "We don't belong together; we never did." There was some truth to that, but I'd managed before. Now I needed proof for what I was about to do.

I wanted to have an affair, if only to see whether I was right about my fantasies. Somewhere during that period, my therapist had said that no self-respecting lesbian would get involved with a straight woman. (When I mentioned this later, she avowed that she didn't say it, but I know she did.) These words kept echoing in my mind. I thought that Bill and I should separate. When I told him this, he was so angry that he kicked a cupboard door, nothing I'd ever seen him do before. It scared me. We tried couples therapy, but he couldn't speak up for himself: he never could. Poor Bill, I think now. How could I have done this to him? I saw his suffering, and I steeled myself against it. What's worse, I even wanted him to *understand* me.

My kids thought that I was crazy, and they were furious at me. My new lesbian friends were egging me on and even some straight friends who'd never understood what I was doing with Bill, anyway. Me, I was driven. I thought that there was a new life, a better life, a truer life, waiting for me out there, if only I were brave enough. I found a summer sublet on the very day that my so-called girlfriend said good-bye.

When I write this now, I think that I was often cruel and stupid. But then I believed that I was right.

Not so long afterward, I was divorced. Bill insisted on it, if I were to leave. And so I managed to buy a house of my own that summer. I hung around with the gay community, primarily on campus, but I didn't have a lover. I kept asking this question in therapy. "Am I a lesbian? Yet? Now?" Her answer was, as usual, opaque. What did I think? What *did* I think? That if I hung out my "For Sale" sign, the ladies would come running?

I'd literally come out of the closet to my non-Boulder friends that summer in Washington, DC, at the first Emily Dickinson

International Society conference. My best women friends, Cris, Jonnie, Martha Nell, and I were drinking wine and gossiping late at night after the conference events, as was our custom. I told them my big news. Everyone was thrilled for me, especially MN, who was a lifelong, very public lesbian. I was sharing Jonnie's free room (she was the conference director), and I was unregistered in the hotel. Suddenly, in our merriment, someone broke a wine glass, which shattered everywhere. "Oh God, we've got to call the hotel to clean it up," Jonnie said. Then she added, "Oh no. They'll see Suzanne and know she doesn't belong in this room!" Our wine-induced logic was a bit fuzzy, for why couldn't I be a guest like the other women? At any rate, someone suggested that I get in the closet when the man came so he wouldn't see me. And I did. He arrived, vacuumed, and left.

"All clear," they called. I opened the sliding door and stepped out.

"She's come out of the closet!" screamed MN. I bowed to everyone. And ever after, this moment was memorialized as my official coming out.

I love this story. I love my EDIS friends and our silliness. But coming out in a DC hotel room to my best long-distance friends had little to do with my life in Boulder. I was meeting lesbians. That was a start. Mostly they were in couples. That was a difficulty. But the main problem, I discovered, was that I had no idea how to come on to a woman. I tried, but I don't think that anyone got it. The process was truly complicated. For one thing, despite the prevailing belief that the categories of "butch" and "femme" were outdated 1950s stereotypes, washed away by granola 1970s feminism when *everybody* wore jeans and hiking boots and didn't shave their armpits, the fact remains that some women were more like what the culture called feminine and some women were more like what the culture considered masculine. In the 1990s, some women wore leather jackets and boots and had short, short hair, and some women wore lipstick and even skirts. I myself loved to play with wearing a tie and a suit jacket. It made me feel cool and gender bending and all those daring things. But I was still feminine in my looks and demeanor. According to cultural clichés of the period, "masculine" women looked like they could be lesbians, but "feminine" women didn't. I was a feminine-looking woman: so how was anyone to know about me?

If I were at a gay gathering, that was a big clue, of course, but I still had no skills for being the one to make overt moves. I knew from my acculturation as a girl and woman how to make the subtler gestures that show a man I am interested, but I didn't technically ever initiate things. I just made space for them to happen. That wasn't working here. Especially because I was attracted to both feminine and masculine women, for I found everyone intriguing as a possible sexual partner.

I made a fool of myself in all sorts of ways, trying to attract straight women who had no idea what I was doing and trying to attract lesbians who were in fact in committed relationships or who just didn't get it. I was also afraid of looking like a fool, so I never went "all out," as it were. Well, I did one time with a straight woman who said she wanted to try, but she never showed up for our assignation. Nothing was happening for me but a lot of frustration. Once someone even set me up on a blind date, but the woman was clearly not anyone whom I wanted to know, so I said I wanted to go home after our dinner—and she was the one person who called me for weeks.

My therapy went on through it all, and there she was, the confident, experienced, partnered "Queen of the Lesbians," as I called her, the woman whom I really loved but who was unavailable for me. So I kept looking for someone who was. I began doing what I did know how to do: planning with my gay university cohorts new courses, maybe a conference, even a program in the new GLB studies. As with feminism twenty years before, a social issue could be an academic issue, too. I had skills that I could confidently offer: my long expertise in academic politics, as well as my leadership skills.

In October, only a few months after it all began, my first romance happened. I met her at a lesbian Halloween costume party, given by that librarian friend to whom I had initially confided my new desires. What to wear? The first question that any girl asks, lesbian or straight. I went down to the Ritz Costume Shop with its dazzling display of costumes and wigs, and I saw—the jodhpurs! They belonged to a World War II uniform, but they were small enough to fit me. Pretty sexy, I thought. But how could they work for this? Then the answer came to me. Which famous lesbian wore jodhpurs? Vita Sackville West, that's who. Famous? Probably no one at this party would have a clue as to who she was, for these were not literary circles. But I knew. Vita: writer, aristocrat, gardener, friend, and possible lover of Virginia Woolf, who lived with her husband Harold Nicolson in what we call today an "open marriage" and who ran off to Paris with Violet Trefusis, another married lady. Vita: who was notorious in the 1920s and 1930s in certain British circles and fascinating to my own world of feminist scholars. Vita: who'd been photographed in a white shirt, boots, and a rope of heirloom pearls with her jodhpurs. Suzanne, get some pearls!

Vita was jaunty, brave, self-assured: she took what she wanted wherever she found it. Suzanne may have been terrified, but as Vita I strode into the party. A room full of Martina Navratilovas and Sapphos. I met; I mingled. I was sitting on the floor talking when suddenly a small attractive woman with dark curly hair, wearing sweats, sat down beside me. "Who are you?" she asked. I had to explain about Vita. "Who are you?" I asked.

"Martina in her warm-ups." She laughed. "Actually I hate costume parties." Her name was Branny (short for Barbara Ann), she taught psychology at Metropolitan State College, and she was definitely a butch woman. We chatted, eagerly, and then as the circle of people moved on to other circles of people, she gave me her phone number on a scrap of paper. Something had happened!

How long to wait before I called? I was back in high school again. I counted a few days, and then I did it: I got in touch. She was very pleased. She came by for a visit, and then there was a long lunch followed by a long walk…She was smart, funny, and one of the most intense people that I've ever met. She lived with a woman, yes, but she said right away that they were not bound to one another sexually. Then came her invitation to a "lesbian Thanksgiving gathering." Her roommate (?) partner (?) was going away that weekend, but others were invited to their mountain home in Nederland. That sounded pretty nice. She said she'd call again to firm up the plans and that she'd pick me up: she already knew that I was a sissy driver.

Three days before Thanksgiving, she called again with the news that her friends had cancelled at the last minute, so it would be just the two of us. Did I mind? "Of course not," I said. "Oh dear," I thought, as I hung up; I thought I knew where this was heading. Did I want to? Could I do it? I didn't feel in love. But I had to go; this was my chance at last. I baked my famous lemon chiffon pie; I bought a split of champagne. And I packed a little overnight bag, just in case. I'd bring it to the car, I plotted, and say that I had my things in case it snowed or something. Later, afterward, she said she'd been worrying how to get me to "bring my things..."

The next morning, she arrived in her jeep. I slipped my little bag onto the back seat, and we drove up the mountain. We turned into a country road until we reached a little red cabin. So pretty, nestled against the mountainside. First we took a long walk down another mountain road, next to a glittering stream. We chattered about something. I was so nervous. I didn't think that she'd be, too—an old hand, as she'd described herself. She'd known that she wanted women since she was a young girl. Her experience was vast, for her youth was spent in the lesbian feminist 1980s. Communal living, the Woman to Woman Bookstore. She had the real credentials. Later I learned that she was indeed nervous, for she'd never been with anyone like me.

After the walk came our dinner. She put a tablecloth on the little table and lit a candle. She was wary of the French champagne. ("Oh Bill, with your wine cellar" came to mind, but I hastily squelched the thought.) She came from an Italian background and had made a family favorite: cauliflower spaghetti. Not your usual Thanksgiving dinner, but then, what was usual about this event? It seemed very romantic to us both.

After dinner, I thought, "Now what?" I thought, "When?" But nothing happened, except that she had a long phone call with her partner who was in New York. Now I was getting worried. Maybe it was too soon in the relationship. Or maybe I'd imagined the whole thing. Or maybe I'd done something wrong. I stood by the window, looking out at the trees, as the sky darkened, and she talked in the other room. At last I heard her come into the living room, and then she was standing behind me. Slowly, she

put her arms around my waist. I turned, and she kissed me. Oh…
"Do you want to?" she asked hesitatingly.

"Oh, yes," I said.

"I didn't know," she said.

"Oh, yes," I said.

"I'll make a fire," she murmured, and she added small logs to the wood burning stove. Before the stove, with its heat to warm us and its light to glow around us, we undressed and then slowly made love. What can I say, more than twenty years later? It was beautiful, everything that I'd imagined. And more, of course, because all I'd ever done was imagine, and this was really happening. A live, warm, lovely woman who wanted me, wanted to make love to me.

Thrilled is the word that describes it best for me. *Shocked* might be another. I felt changed, somehow. We slept that night in the little guest room off the living room. It happened again, and I did my part more avidly. I was filled with joy.

The next day after breakfast, we drove down the mountain, but only to pick up more of my things so I could spend the weekend in the little cabin with her. An idyll, it seemed to me. But then real life, in the form of her partner, returned. For the other woman *was* her partner, and she did not take kindly to the turn of events. Sex with someone else was okay, it turned out, but falling in love was not. Through December and January, Branny and I were quite simply having an affair, except that it was not secret, and her partner was angry and jealous, as usually happens. But we saw each other; we spoke on the phone. She commuted to her work in Denver on the bus. She would pull into my driveway in the morning with her cheery grin, wearing a dashing cap, on her way to the Park and Ride, and often I'd meet her return bus, just to see her.

Branny was ten years younger than I am, born in the early 1950s. Political to the core, she'd done it all: civil rights, feminism, gay rights. She'd lived in a commune and on a Native American reservation, worked in an abortion clinic and a women's bookstore. She had an MA in social psychology and was an instructor at Metropolitan State College in Denver. She was intelligent and funny. She loved birds and all other animals.

Despite our obvious differences—class turned out to be the most significant, as she had a working-class background—there was much to bind us, as well: intelligence, feminism, and a romantic spirit. I called her my "gentilesse knight," a phrase cribbed from Chaucer: I loved her devoted ways. Despite her rough demeanor, she was sweet and good. My love grew.

There is a famous lesbian joke. Q: "What does a lesbian bring on the first date?" A: "A U Haul with all her possessions in it." Everyone knew the joke. *We* would never do anything like that, we told one another. But her situation at home grew untenable, and in February she moved in with me. Except for a few separations along the years, always resulting in reunions, we have been together ever since.

And the therapist? That relationship continued as before, with a new subject for discussion. Of course, Branny was jealous of the therapist, but I was adamant. Two loves had I. One in "real life," "one in the floating world of therapy." I lived my lesbian life. The conference was held, and the courses were invented; my own research shifted to what was first LGB studies, then LBGT studies, and finally queer theory, and we were able to establish a program in the College of Arts and Sciences.

Branny is my official domestic partner. Were we "meant for each other"? What does that mean after all? After twenty years, passionate romance morphs once and once again. We have *our* life, with its rituals, customs, and sticking points. We are together. We love one another.

In my life I have never reached that young girl's goal of a perfect true love, a perfect soul mate, and I now know how much of a fantasy that is. Today, a primary relationship with a woman suits me well, as does physical love with a woman. But I have learned that my fantasies about lesbian love had been as idealized as my earlier beliefs about what I would find in heterosexual love. Sex and gender are not the only elements that define how relationships develop, what shapes they take, or how they work or don't. There are pleasures and problems in any form of intimacy. I have had three marriages, each one a gift, for I no longer disown my relationships with men, as I thought I must do when I was first identifying myself as a lesbian. I truly loved those men, no matter that I might well have had erotic stirrings in my relationships with women even then, even earlier, feelings that I never understood. When I looked at those feelings and acknowledged them, I changed my life, but they are not my only truth. I struggled to find the true love of romance all of my life, and I have made many dramatic changes on behalf of this goal. In the end, although true love has been a chimera, I think that I have been a lucky woman, because I have had serious loves, and all of them were real.

Coda

That woman is no longer my therapist, and I no longer love her. But I can see how this heightened awareness between two people was commensurate with some aspects of romantic love, as I understood it: communicating the deepest and most important feelings and experiences and feeling fully alive. I came to this therapy as a person always longing for romance. And I got it, all of it: the suffering as well as the heights. I repeated all those scenarios that I'd acted out forever, only this time I got to *talk* about them. I found out where they came from, why they had never gone away, and what they meant.

After eight years, she left Boulder suddenly to take a job in another city. This was a very abrupt ending to our relationship. She tried to prepare me in those few months between her announcement and her departure, but I never was truly prepared. Probably the time was too short for what still needed to be done. The transference was not resolved, as they say in psychoanalytic parlance, and even after all that time and work, I did not create a new and more usable pattern for loving her. Therefore, the feelings for her did not die. She remained in my mind a beloved whom I could not have and in this way repeated, rather than altered, the paradigm itself that I had known since my childhood.

But there is more to the story. For I found a new therapist, with whom I did *not* fall in love. I did not want to do this ever again. And so she became for me a different kind of mother figure, one whom I began to love without all the drama, the longing. Of course we talked at length about that recent transference love, which by this time was focused on the bitterness of betrayal. Then one day my new therapist asked, "Why would you keep on wanting more of it, when it led to such suffering? Why would you not prefer what you have here, where there is no pain?"

It was an extraordinary moment. "What I have *here*?" She was saying, I believe, that in this therapy I was exploring my life issues without repeating them. How could this be? Because she also seemed to be saying that she was an appropriate object for the kind of love that I did have for her. "Do you care for me?" I then asked.

"Yes," she said.

That moment seemed to release me. It was amazing how quickly the flame of the torch that I was carrying for my former therapist flickered and went out. I was loving a mother-figure in a new way, and I was happy in this love.

This new way was calmer and steadier, based in a paradigm different from my childhood heritage, which was a love that came and went and consequently fostered romantic drama. Therapy taught me the term "conditional love" to describe this situation. Its opposite is "unconditional love": a love that accepts another person for who she is and does not require conditions. These two terms helped me to understand the lure of the story of true love, which promises a great love that will last forever, the ultimate in unconditional love.

Then I thought about the loves that I have known in my adult life with people who loved me after the violins had ceased their music: people who offered love in ways that lasted despite changes in external situations, another aspect of "unconditional"— Joseph, Bill, Branny. At last I started to see something about the forms that love can take and to appreciate them.

Today, after a long life, I believe that my quest for that one great love has stilled. Romance is not necessarily true love, and true love does not always mean forever after. There are so many good ways to love.

This is not a therapy fairy tale, however. I am not a totally different woman. I haven't let go of a lot of my old patterns, and I doubt that I ever will. I still ask for more in my relationships than many people want to give. I still hurt when they leave, as many do. And I confess that I am not over my delight in love stories: I still like a happy ending. But these days I take those stories with a grain of salt. Irony helps; humor helps. Knowing that they are stories helps. I really do think that I care as much about "love" as Suzy Hecht did, but today I understand so much more about its complexity than she ever could.

PART IV

Working Woman

10

Opening the Door to Academia

On a June night in 2008, I was the guest of honor at an elegant dinner party, hosted by my daughter Jenny. My family and closest friends sat around me at small tables, eating delicious food, laughing, chatting. I was glowing. We were celebrating my retirement. Later, champagne and delectable desserts were served outside on the patio. An air of festivity floated on the breezes. Everyone looked beautiful. There were lovely toasts. Later, my granddaughter Eliza, then eight, serenaded us with a song of her own composition on her brand-new guitar. What a happy and memorable night. I kept calling it my graduation party.

I was eager to leave my life as professor of English at CU. The disappointment and unhappiness that had propelled my decision were behind me, and I was full of hope.

When I look back at my life as an English professor and the experiences that led to my retirement, I see how my personal story has actually much to do with the fact that I am a member of the first generation of women's studies scholars. I worked on women's issues in the university throughout my career and wrote about them in my scholarship, focusing primarily on women writers. How I managed to forge a successful career and the kinds of prices that I paid to do this, along with the pride that I took in it, are a part of the history of feminist women that was made in the late twentieth century and on into the twenty-first.

At the end, my early retirement and desire to leave the world of the university behind me was still connected to my gender politics. I did not understand that then, for as feminists working to change the academy we had never given much thought to what would happen during a woman's later years. We needed to focus on getting women into the profession and trying to keep them there. Yet I now can see the whole arc of my career and my retirement as a piece of that story, at once illustrative and a tale unique to me.

When I joined the University of Colorado as an assistant professor in 1974, I was so excited to have a "real job," a tenure track position, after five years of trying. I was hired to teach American literature with a specialty in American poetry. As a new feminist, I had taught two courses in women's literature when I was working as an instructor in various institutions. One was at Bucknell University in Pennsylvania as a one-time-only "university course" with my friend Amy Kaminsky, an instructor in Spanish. We had to make a special application for our class in American and Spanish women writers, since we were only instructors. The other was at San Jose State University, where another faculty member was kind enough to "loan" me her women and literature course: there I taught women's poetry for the first time.

When I came to CU, I discovered that there was a move afoot to establish a program in women's studies. This was a radical idea. I threw myself into the endeavor and met women as passionate as I was about making the study of women an academic enterprise. I was proud to be elected to the newly formed board. To give a sense of the times, I often tell the story of when I first suggested courses on women and literature to the English department. Someone at the conference table suggested snidely that the course should be taught "out on Thirteenth Street," so un-academic was it perceived to be. But finally they did let me try it out, and the thrill of working with students to read this new material was heady—new because there were hardly any women writers on any course syllabi at all. Then came discovering how to study it and how it had meaning both personal, academic, and political: these could all go together, we learned. "The personal is the political" was after all the rallying cry of 1970s feminism. The classroom was a vital place, alive with excitement, as together the students and I read writing by women, both known in academia, like Emily Dickinson and the Brontës, and unknown, like the poet Adrienne Rich. There were almost no women writers on most literature syllabi. Even Dickinson, who had written 1,755 poems, was known by about fifteen or twenty of them.

I was a bright-eyed new assistant professor, proud of myself for getting there and loving it all. Well, most of it. The classroom wasn't always easy for me, no matter that I loved teaching. In some of my traditional courses, it was hard to earn respect. I didn't look like a professor: I was too young, and I was a woman. There were very few women professors when I came in 1974 and for many years after. Once, after I'd finished the opening class of a course, I asked as usual if there were any questions. A young man raised his hand and asked, "What are your credentials to teach this course? "Another time, when I came in to start a class, a fellow at the back of the room was reading a newspaper, with his legs on the chair in front of him. He kept on reading as I spoke, so finally I asked him to put down the paper, for the class had begun. "Oh, I thought you were still telling jokes," he said.

The large English department was not exactly a welcoming place. I remember sitting at department meetings wanting to hide under my chair, as older male faculty fought bitterly and downright cruelly with one another over department politics. In later years, when I was an older faculty member, I saw junior women faculty cringing with the same fear, and I would try to calm them afterward by saying, "They're just beating their chests to hear themselves talk." But these men were loud and often mean, and there was no getting past that.

There were only two women in the department when I came, and they had both been beaten down by the system and by their so-called colleagues. One had become an alcoholic, and the other would rarely show her face in the department except to teach her classes. I would be different, I vowed. I would win.

It took me a while, but I finally developed a system for participating in department meetings. Initially, if I voiced a suggestion or an opinion, it was simply ignored. Who was I, after all? So I figured out that I could actually use my training as a conventional female, much as it galled me. I would ask an innocent question. "Why do we *need* a new course on composition?" Or "What are the regulations for firing someone from a committee?" The battle would rage, and in this way my (unvoiced) opinion would be brought into the discussion. Later, as I achieved more seniority in rank and years, I had fewer compunctions about speaking more openly, but participating in university-wide politics *always* required a degree of deviousness. I confess that I never ceased worrying about what people thought of me.

(This was in the early 1970s. It is unnerving to have recently read an op-ed piece in the *New York Times* from January 9, 2015, by Sheryl Sandburg and Adam Grant. Grant is a professor of business. Sandburg is the author of the quasifeminist book *Lean In: Women, Work, and the Will to Lead,* which purports to teach women how to achieve leadership positions in business. This piece, devoted to women's difficulty in speaking up in meetings, suggests that leaders—who are still primarily men—must take steps to encourage women to speak and be heard. Is this sexist? No comment.)

When after six years I came up for tenure and promotion to associate professor, I had written not only the requisite book but two books, for I had published the first before I was even hired in my years without a real job. The first was on a conventional topic, metaphor in modern long poems, the subject of my dissertation—all male poets, of course. But the new book was on American women poets. That was a little dicey. I had also published articles and had given papers and lectures across the country, primarily on women writers. "You're lucky that you have *more* than most people," said the chair(man) of my promotion committee, "because there's going to be a problem about the subject of most of your work." He added, "Plus, I'm going to need to address the rumor that you don't like men in your classes." (!)

I got my promotion, although the vote was far from unanimous.

Four years later in 1984, unusually soon for this next step (the average is six to eight years), I was promoted to full professor, for by then I had written two more books: *Emily Dickinson and the Space of the Mind,* and an edited volume, *Feminist Critics Read Emily Dickinson.* I was forty-two. I had made it. Not only was I young for this promotion but I was a woman, the first woman full professor not only in my department but also in the university at large. (Even today, forty years later, women full professors are rare.) Plus I was writing about women. How did I do it? Because in this system, although one's work is always critiqued, in the end what matters most are numbers: how many books, how many articles. My training and inclination as a writer are primarily what made it happen for me. I like to write books.

Now I look back at my career, particularly at CU where I taught for thirty-eight years. Why the anger, resentment, and disappointment that prompted my retirement when I was a success?

Full professor is the top rung of the long ladder that academics must climb in our profession. One test after another. Our lives and careers flourish or fail by passing these tests or not. Some make it, many don't. After full professor, then what? There existed some routes to further advancement that I did not or felt I could not take. First, I did not move on to a better institution, as many do, a common method for advancement. Unlike most women professors, I was a mother and a wife, raising a family in Boulder, and I felt that this was not possible for me. Second, there were no Endowed Chairs in the Humanities at CU. Finally I did not take administrative positions. I never even became the chair of my very large department, though as a full professor I should have taken my turn. This was primarily because I couldn't imagine giving up my writing for four years. I realize now that that this decision was probably foolhardy, for I did not enter the world of university power: chairs and deans.

I simply continued my work, moving into new and interesting areas of scholarship, publishing more and more books and articles. I authored or coauthored seven more books and wrote a total of forty-two articles. I presented lectures and papers in the

United States and internationally. I helped to found the Emily Dickinson International Society in 1980 and was the first editor of *The Emily Dickinson Journal* for ten years. I was especially noted as a Dickinson specialist, though I worked on other subjects as well. At CU I helped found the women's studies major, then the gender studies program. Later, in the '90s, I was on the founding committee for the Gay, Lesbian, Bisexual Certificate Program, as it was called then.

But despite my success in the academic world at large, it seemed to me that I never achieved senior *stature* at my own institution. I thought that my senior rank would make me an esteemed member of the CU community. For example, I would have been asked to sit on more prestigious university committees, such as search committees for new presidents. But this kind of thing did not happen, and I grew confused and frustrated. I thought that it was something about me, that I was, well, unlikable.

Only in retrospect have I begun to understand more about my experiences as a full professor. I think that they reveal yet another stage in the career trajectory of academic women. As I have said, none of us had every considered this issue back when we, the first generation of feminist scholars, began our work on behalf of women in academia in the 1970s, toiling all those years to make it possible for there to *be* anything like a body of academic women and for them, God forbid, to flourish. We were busy working on hiring, tenuring, promoting, salarying for women, as they moved (or did not) through the system. We thought that to be a full professor was winning the prize. We had no idea that there might be barriers confronting us after we reached the goal, that bias against women in our profession, especially at individual institutions, does not go away—especially when most of my work on campus and off challenged the sexist, racist, homophobic institution at its core. I was defiantly *not* one of the boys, and the boys ran the show.

It is true that the profession began to change *because* of the work in which I and my cohorts engaged over the decades: affirmative action in hiring (which did not simplistically mean hiring people of color, as people think of it today), equal pay for women and minorities (we never could fix the salary inequity), and academic courses about people other than "dead white males." Slowly, people other than white men infiltrated the ranks of the faculty.

(I've checked recent statistics, however, and they reveal that even today these "others" are clustered primarily in the junior ranks of the professoriate; there are still very few women full professors in American universities and colleges; there is still significant gender difference in promotion to tenure and associate professor, even though many more women are hired at the assistant professor rank than in my time. Women spend longer at the associate professor level than do men. In the sciences, the situation is direr at all ranks. Plus, even as the number of adjunct, part-time faculty with PhDs has grown everywhere, the number of women in this situation is far greater. Women continue to "leave" the profession all along the way. They don't get tenure; they get "stalled" at the associate rank. In various ways all along the career path, they don't seem to meet the standards, even now. Why not? What interferes with women's progress?)

In 1984, I knew only that the situation had to be changed and that I wanted to be among those who would change it. I liked this work; I liked my feminist cohorts, who worked in many departments and fields of study. We all felt united in a cause that mattered. Our differences on issues were productive and actually made us smarter and stronger. We developed an intimacy that one did not feel in the Department of English.

We established a group called Women for Equity on campus. We fought on all fronts. I served frequently on college promotion committees so that I could bring up issues of gender there: for example, as a reason why women didn't publish "enough." I suggested that their more intense involvement with teaching and nurturing students had a great deal to do with their acculturation as women and that the standards for promotion should take this into account. I always lost, but at least the issue was raised. In later years, feminists themselves would label such a stance "essentialist," but I still think that society hasn't changed enough for this not to be a factor. Statistics reveal that the prime issue to this day for women's career trajectory in the university is childcare. Childcare is still women's responsibility in most families, and women with children have more difficulties with promotion issues—and, in general, simply staying in the profession.

Why "*women's* poetry?" I would be asked when I first taught this class, but usually the phrase that people used was "feminine poetry." "Feminine?" Because for one thing, women writers were not published as frequently as men. They often chose personal and nontraditional subjects, like sex or even menstruation, or wrote about subjects that were not considered appropriate for women, like politics or war. We also wanted to see if women wrote differently about traditional subjects and, if they even *wrote* differently, in terms of style or language. There was and still is much to study.

Teaching such material was educational, and it was exciting. It made for intense and wide-ranging discussion, when we could study form, style, subject matter, and so forth, bringing to bear scholarship and personal knowledge. In addition, studying the poetry opened up wider social issues, such as the role of women as a group in society and the importance of difference—class, race, and sexual preference—among women. Slowly, as courses like this became understood to have academic content and scholarship itself proliferated, we were able to make them part of the general college curriculum, and the field of Women's Studies was born. Today students don't even realize that there was a problem: they think that Women's Studies always existed and that women writers were *always* taught in English classes!

In the early 1990s, a wave of new possibility infused my CU world, as the struggle for what was then called gay rights surfaced. Even as the Women's Movement of the 1970s or the Black Movement of the 1960s had led to academic involvement, so what was originally called LGB (then LGBT) Studies became a possibility. I was in my early fifties and had recently come out as a lesbian. With fervor I joined the existing campus groups and helped to start the academic wing of the movement. We held a scholarly conference on campus in 1994. We formed an LGBT Studies Committee in 1997 to study existing programs in the country and then convince the dean that we might have a program at CU. Ultimately, we began as a Certificate Program. In English we created two LBG courses, and I taught them. The old thrill of discovery was heightened for me when I learned a whole new body of material: novels and poetry by gay men. My own scholarship reflected my interest in these subjects, and as LGBT turned to "queer," I was right there.

This work was even more disturbing to the wider community than Women's Studies twenty years earlier. Right after the program was initiated, for example, a parent, enraged that his child had enrolled in a course called Introduction to LGBT Studies, went straight to the top and called a member of the Board of Regents to complain. Soon afterward, I found myself at a special Regents Meeting at the State Capitol. Right before we were to go in, the chancellor leaned across the table where we were having coffee and said to me, "Now what exactly *is* 'transgender'?" I was happy to help him out.

From my story thus far, it is obvious that as a feminist I focused my work in the classroom, on committees, and in my writing on social change. These activities in academia reflected what was happening in society at large, and many of us believed that the university, the place where the young were educated, was a prime location for this work to happen.

But as times moved on from my start in the 1970s, something unfortunate happened. Our student body itself changed, as others besides me will attest. Students grew more generally conservative, and worse, they felt a strong sense of entitlement. Everything that was not working in the classroom was the professor's fault, as the students sat in increasing judgment. As for me, they did not like my feminism; they did not like my sexual preference. They did not like my age, even as older woman occupy a tenuous position in society at large. This was the final stage of my gendered position in the classroom. When I started, I was a young woman and had to prove myself as a person who could stand in front of the class. Then I was a middle-aged woman, whom students frequently understood as more like a mother figure than a professor. Then I was an older woman, and my classroom status as "professor" dropped accordingly. So different from the white-haired gentlemen who automatically were authorities.

I am not speaking about every student, not at all. As a teacher in all of my courses, my expansive personality and deep beliefs had always bothered some students as much as they excited others, and this continued, but the group in the middle grew larger. Even English majors in a senior seminar called Women's Poetry and Feminist Theory turned out by the twenty-first century not to "believe" in feminism. What were they doing there? My only answer is to surmise that senior seminars are required for the major, and maybe the class time was right. It was a painful semester. Picture ten people sitting around a table, staring back at me silently half of the time and by the end of the semester refusing even to answer my questions.

I took it personally, although advised by many not to do so. "It's just a job," they told me. But I was dismayed. I tried to teach better. I tried to teach differently. I tried to please them—the kiss of death really, for really good teaching. I talked about it in therapy. A lot. But really, I didn't know how to teach any other way. To me, personal connection *meant* teaching. I was advised to offer nonfeminist classes, like American Literary Masterpieces. But how could I keep my feminism or sexual politics out of studying Hemingway *or* Dickinson? The result of all of these factors was that my experience of the classroom kept turning into a sense of disgrace. I began to dread entering the room.

As for status in the university, I think that I lost that chance when, as I've said, I did not serve as chair. But I was asked to serve on one important committee: the Vice Chancellor's Promotion and Tenure Committee, the final step up the university ladder and where the real decisions are made. My earlier work on the college committee helped here, plus the fact that by then they needed full professors who were women and minorities. Although that committee required an enormous amount of work, I willingly did it because of my commitment to representing the situations and needs of persons other than white heterosexual males. Also, since the majority of the committee members were scientists, teaching them something about how success in the Humanities worked was a major task. This committee had power, for it made the decision on the issues that counted—that is, people's jobs.

In the end, I see that I had, after all, cast myself from the beginning as an outsider, as much as I wanted to be an insider. I wanted to belong, but I wanted to challenge. I needed to challenge. There was too much at stake for the world, I thought, for someone in my privileged position not to use it to change "the system." As a young feminist, I used to stand in front of my classes and say, "It does no good to opt out: to live on a commune and take up basket weaving. We should be inside the system to change it." To do so, I understood, you had to follow the rules as much as possible so that you could be there to change them. You had to be promoted, to become a full professor. You had to publish.

Some women couldn't understand this or didn't want to do it. "I came here to teach," they said. "I have children to raise," they said. "I need to follow my husband to his new job," they said. The system didn't care. "Publish," it demanded, "and not just anywhere. Not in those hand-printed journals called *Womyn*; those aren't real." But for all who faltered along the way or dropped out completely, there were others like myself who made it. I was driven; I was gifted; I was savvy.

A few years before I made the decision to retire, I took a final stab at achieving university-wide honor. I asked my department chair to recommend me for the university distinguished professor rank. The department, then the college, did recommend me, though I was warned about being a humanist, when all the distinguished professors were famous scientists. I waited on tenterhooks for the decision. When it came, it was bizarre. I was told, not no exactly, but to come back next year. Why? Because, they said, my outside letters of recommendation did not come from "good enough" institutions—even though, whether the assembled DPs making the decision knew it or not, they came from the most distinguished scholars in the field in which I was most well known: Dickinson Studies. No one said outright, "We are all men but one; we are all scientists, and naturally none of us of do research on women or gays." But on the other hand, it was clear even to them that, given what I do, I do it very well. Hence, I suppose, the inability to "just say no." But I got the message: "You don't fit into our club." This was the message that I'd been trying to surmount for forty years in the academy.

I do realize, however, that despite my feminist analysis of my situation, I did not have to react exactly as I did. Women full professors besides me exist, and they do not all turn tail and run. True, many of my friends hold Endowed Professorships, with the perks and honor attendant upon such a position, but none were available in the Humanities at CU. Some of my friends teach at schools where the number of students truly interested in learning is higher. Some have different personalities from mine. They are calmer, less emotional. Some are humbler, not desiring fame so much. Some are less needy. They don't want love from their students or, God forbid, from their colleagues—much less from their institution. Some differ from me in other ways. But this is my story.

I did not apply for the distinguished professorship the next year. What I did was leave. I arranged to retire. I signed the papers, packed up my books, turned in my keys.

Later in the month in the moonlight, at her party, her graduation party, with a small group of friends and family, Mom/Grammy/Suzanne did feel beloved and proud, especially when her three daughters toasted her, even calling her a role model. Proud and ready to go forth into a new world of her own making.

11

A Love for Language: My Legacy

At the University of Colorado, we used the categories teaching, service, and scholarship to define our activities. For me, the best part of my job was the scholarship component: research, writing, and publication. I like to read about books, write about books, and publish my writing about books. Basically, I like books. Teaching others about them means a lot to me. But I believe that my greatest skill and gift is my writing, and so the writing requirement of my profession suited me well. At CU, I was in the middle of my life and my work and had no thought of legacy. That has come much later, after I retired. It should not be a surprise, however, that my lifelong love for language has entered into my contemplations about the possibility of a legacy.

I have written my way through my professional life in all kinds of personal weather: marriage, divorce, trauma, and celebration. "How could you?" people would ask. I watched so many of my colleagues struggle to write, when the more immediate demands of a class or a meeting or "life" came first. "How could I not?" I thought, for it is writing that sustains me, and I find it even more necessary in difficult days. The fact that I have written and published so much has to do, of course, with the rewards that accrued for this: promotion, raises, and reputation, and this is not insignificant. But primarily, I think that this happened because writing matters so much to me, and I need to do it. Writing has always been central in my life. I was a writer of poetry and stories before I became a scholar, and I intend to be a writer for all of my life.

The writing process is one of the most satisfying experiences that I know. I am in love with language. I love the pliability of words and sentences and the process of finding just the right word for the sentence that I am making, finding just the right sentence, so that I can give a form to my ideas and in this way share them with others. (I just considered "malleable" and "manipulable" before settling on "pliable," for example.) This is work, but it is exciting. Language is powerful, and it can change the world, I really believe—or the particular portion of it that I am trying to reach.

Another aspect of writing that matters deeply to me is that, although writing is a private and solitary activity, at the same time it places me in a special kind of relationship. "I" seek words by listening to "myself," an entity with whom I am in an internal dialogue: "Does this work? Does this sound right? Is it apt? Inadequate? Good?" I ask "myself." The other "I" listens to those words and then responds with affirmation or criticism, with suggestions. We work together, and I feel in the presence of an aspect of myself who knows me and sustains me. When writing, I always feel both alive and content: my best self.

My heart stops racing, I settle into the page (as I still think of it). I may be safe here, but that doesn't mean that I am not working like crazy. Writing is difficult, and I like that part of it, too. Every sentence is a stretch to achieve, the result of an interaction between the words as they form and the idea in the back of my head, my sense of what this is supposed to be about, guiding my progress even as it is constantly redefined by what actually gets said. This, too, is a relationship, an aspect of what I am trying to describe when I speak about "me" and "me" working in tandem.

In graduate school, there appeared in my life someone who also became a part of my writing process from that time on. My advisor Josephine Miles saw not simply the fact that I was intelligent and clever, for she lived in a world of very smart people, but she recognized the particular nature of my mind. Her great gift to me was that she found it and me valuable.

Miss Miles, as she was called, was a scholar and poet, the only woman professor at Berkeley when I was there in the 1960s, a professor who chose me among many to be her student. You did not ask her: she asked you. She was the most intelligent person whom I have ever known and also the humblest. She listened. She thought that there was something to learn from her students and others. Yet her mind was formidable and her standards were rigorous. Her writing was astute and precise; with her, no word was out of place. Nothing short of the best would do, for her own work and for others. For mine. Even after I left her presence and after she left this life,

I have felt her leaning over my shoulder as I write and saying, "You can do better than this." Today I still try to write every sentence in accordance with her standards.

Writing is slow and frustrating as well as exhilarating and even joyful. Many writers before me have talked about feeling good if they get a few paragraphs written in a day. If you labor over a sentence, it isn't even really finished. Not then, not the day after. Maybe next week (or next year)! Revision is always necessary: everything looks different when you step away. Writing is work: that's the point. But work is fine. Work is good. It makes you feel that you're meant for something: you have a reason to be on the planet. And working in relationship, if it's me and me, or me and Miss Miles, or later yet, me and an editor, is the best way to work. Always, relationality helps me to enter a place of self-knowledge.

My profession gave me the opportunity to indulge in my favorite kind of work. And so I responded to the mandate to research, write, and publish with enthusiasm and dedication for over thirty years. I did not find it a chore, as some do, but an opportunity: I was paid for this.

Yet it was not poetry or fiction or autobiography that I was required to write, but literary criticism, and this is a special skill in its own right. My work as an academic critic did not come easily to me at first. I learned my trade, but I was always a bit of a maverick in that endeavor, and I usually had to fight to get those books and essays published. Why? This is the story that I need to tell.

To explain what I consider to be the source of my ideas about scholarly writing, I have to go back to my undergraduate education, to Bennington College. I have explained how Bennington was a progressive college, where a student's independence and participation in the makeup of her own education were central to the college's principals. Bennington's philosophy was formed in large part by the educational theories of John Dewey.

Dewey was also noteworthy for his ideas about art, his emphasis on the concept of "art as experience" (1934). He believed in the continuity of art with everyday life, meaning that the individual art object served as a conduit through which an artist and an active observer encountered one another and in the process participated in the culture at large. Bennington focused on the arts, and I went there because I wanted to be an actor and a writer. I took classes in acting, dance, creative writing, drawing, sculpture, and even printmaking, as well as more academic subjects. But ultimately, I became a professional scholar who studied art instead. However, even in a standard course on, for example, literature or art history, at Bennington Dewey's ideas about the function of art prevailed. I now see that his more encompassing idea—that the aesthetic experience is central to human meaning—became basic to my own beliefs about the profound significance of art in culture. This belief has persisted throughout my life, notwithstanding the various other aesthetic theories that I necessarily encountered in a very long career.

I took these ideas from Bennington to the more traditional education that I received at Berkeley and then on into my career in the academy. I see now how my untraditional ideas about how I did literary criticism, something that I always identified with my essential "creativity," had also to do with Dewey's ideas. Basically, I believe that art is an important and powerful component of society, not an elitist plaything or "extra." How this transferred to my own writing has not just to do with my primary approach to literature and gender politics, but with the form that my language has taken. One aspect of that form is clarity. Rather than writing in the scholarly speak that became more and more stylish in the academy, I chose to write in the form that came more naturally to me: ordinary language. I wanted all people to be able to understand my work.

I was given the tools to emphasize language itself in my study of literature in graduate school. There I was trained in New Criticism, or formalism, which meant focusing on the art object, the poem or novel or story, so as to understand its structure. "Close reading" of a literary text gave one an understanding of how it was made, its language patterns, vocabulary, syntax, and so forth, and how that helped to create meaning. Dewey, too, was concerned about understanding the aesthetic object, which he did not see as contradictory to understanding its place in society. I was convinced that knowing as much as one could about the work of art would help the reader form a connection with it and that this would give her or him tools for appreciating and enjoying it more thoroughly and also for seeing art's centrality to life.

This set of beliefs persisted through the constant changing of the guard, as it were: the theories that dominated English departments over the decades, from historicism to structuralism to deconstructionism to cultural construction to new historicism and all the other isms that had their day in my forty years as a literary critic. I learned them all, but I never changed my basic beliefs, even when more and more the current *theory* seemed to become more important than the work of art itself.

This caused problems for me in various ways. Because I believed that literature was written for "real" people and not scholars, I insisted on making complicated ideas accessible, particularly in the face if the growing abstruseness of high theory. However, the idea that if you could understand the writing, then it wasn't smart, became the prevailing thought in my field. Thus, my first book, *Metaphor and the Poetry of Williams, Pound, and Stevens*, was rejected by one press because the reviewer said that it was too simple, "more suited for an undergraduate audience." I am lucky that another press did publish it and subsequent generations of readers have appreciated it.

How I wept in the 1980s because I couldn't write like priestesses such as Judith Butler and Julia Kristeva in the super intellectual language that dominated my field. True, I could and did make their theories available to students and professors who didn't teach at Yale or Berkeley, people who would come up to me at conferences and say, "I love your work because I can *understand* it." But writing as I did, I could not become a truly famous scholar. "Do you want to write like that? I'll bet you could if you tried," said my husband.

"Well no, I don't. It's *wrong*," I replied.

"There you have it," he said. I was doomed to my lesser stature: heroine in Des Moines, bust at Yale.

When I was about to retire and asked to give the address to parents and students at the English department's graduation ceremony, the topic of my talk was very different from any that I had ever heard over the years, as professors would declaim something analytic about their own academic specialty on that occasion. "What do these parents *care*?" I would think. I myself talked about the purpose of an English major. I said that it gave the students the gift of reading well, with insight and skill, so that they could increase their experience of the pleasure and meaning of literature throughout their lives. This approach had little to do with what I'd experienced in my profession for forty years.

My Bennington education emerged in other ways, as well. I persisted in following my scholarly interests to answer different questions about writing and reading that became pressing to me. I strayed across historical periods and disciplines, using an eclectic merging of perspectives, including feminism, queer theory, and psychoanalysis. This habit made it difficult (but not impossible) for me to publish my work in the university world of strict historical periods and methodologies. My Bennington training in independent thinking was far more central to my approach to my work than staying in those prescribed boxes. It also trained me to value originality in my thinking, rather than staying content to tweak the scholarship of others.

In graduate school after my PhD exam, Jo Miles invited me and my family to her home. We sat on her patio, and she toasted me with champagne. "You are so funny," she chuckled, thinking of the three-hour grilling that I had undergone. "Someone could ask you which way was North, and you'd think that you had to figure it out for yourself." Oh, Bennington.

Bennington also influenced my writing style itself. In graduate school, I was taught that there was only one format for writing an academic essay: thesis, argument, conclusion, all argued in an impersonal tone. In my first year in graduate school, I had a professor who'd spent a Fulbright year at Bennington. He knew that I had gone there, and in his class in Victorian Literature, when he gave our first paper assignment, he paced around the seminar table, saying, "We will not illustrate this paper. We will not dance this paper. We will *write* this paper." That was meant for me, of course—the girl who'd had an education where all of these forms of writing "papers" were not only possible but encouraged.

I didn't dance the books and papers that I wrote (although once Cristanne Miller and I, interested in the topic of performance and poetry, gave a talk where we each played the part of a poem, with the other as the reader asking questions of the poem), but I did permit—indeed, encourage—my own voice to emerge as the speaker of my essays. At times I chose to include the forbidden word "I" or even personal experience, if I thought that they added something to my idea. In my last book, which was about relationships between women that were established by way of writing and reading, I even included some illustrations, photos of those greeting cards that I'd made for my mother.

When I am writing criticism, I am like most critics creating an argument to make my ideas convincing to the reader. I, too, have a thesis, topic sentences, and a conclusion. But this does not preclude allowing my own voice to come through in a way that we were taught not to do in graduate school. We were to keep ourselves out of the text, to write pseudoscience, as it were, so that the writing was neutral and did not get in the argument. But I believe (Bennington again?) that the literary argument is a) not science and b) that it is stronger when the reader gets a sense that a person is making it: "God is not writing this paper, I am," I used to say.

When I write about literature, my practice has been akin to what I think of as putting my ear to the text, the better to hear it speak. I see myself as an interlocutor, using my skills to share what I find there. I am not naïve about this. "What I find" is a loaded concept, and the same poem can evoke many, many interpretations. But I have believed that if you measure an interpretation against the words before you, recognizing your own values and purposes and testing them against the words themselves, you can come closer, at any rate, to touching the text. For example, in the case of a poet like Emily Dickinson, many interpretations do make sense, because the poem is rich, complex, and playful enough to contain such multiplicity. But for my part, if I try to read that poem as humbly as I can and give what I find to my reader, then I think that we might share the poem in a way that enlarges our own minds and honors the work of art. From this position, feminist theory or psychoanalytic theory or whatever set of ideas that I am employing are not the focus: they are the tools. As author, I want to establish a common ground with my reader to promote a conversation of sorts.

But my style and frequently my intent often got me into professional trouble. They were too different from the norm, and I emerged as a bit of a maverick, as I've said, no matter how good I was. Still, I sought recognition, and I didn't really want to be an oddball. But in retrospect I find that I cherish my ways of doing this work, no matter that they have complicated my professional journey, and I am proud of being a "Bennington girl." I like the way that I think, even if it wasn't entirely suited for great prominence in my profession. It enabled me to share my ideas in a form that made sense to me and to many others.

When I retired after forty years and deliberately left the academic life, the person called "Suzanne Juhasz" seemed to me to have become a ghost. I could not help but wonder: Has she simply gone, or might she have left behind a legacy? What I gave to my own university is clear to me. What about beyond it? For a book is not a public lecture or even a class. There is no literal audience, so no matter how much I believe that a relationship does exist between author and reader, it is one that happens in the mind only. Apart from a few reviews and citations and a few comments at conferences, I really have no knowledge of who has read my writing, much less who has liked it or found it meaningful. The matter of "legacy" has been worrisome.

This is especially so because for me retirement has meant entering worlds where I have been just a person, someone without fame or recognition. I did not know if "Suzanne Juhasz" has lingered behind me. But then, in the last few years, I have had experiences that suddenly made the idea of legacy a possibility.

Although I stopped participating in conferences or attending lectures, there was one organization that I didn't leave. EDIS, the Emily Dickinson International Society, is still "mine." I helped to found it thirty years ago. It is more than just a scholarly organization, for its members include both academics and people who have nothing to do with universities but who love Dickinson's poetry. We created our society so that it would mingle these groups. EDIS means companionship and even fun—and lots of good food. I have dear and very old friends there and newer friends, as well.

At these gatherings, I began to discover something about "Suzanne Juhasz." Sometimes young people from the United States and even other nations have looked at my nametag, and I have seen their eyes light up. "Oh, you're Suzanne Juhasz! I'm so excited to meet you," they say. Often they have told me that they've used my work in their dissertations or essays. When I ask what work of mine in particular, they frequently say *The Undiscovered Continent.* That is my first book, written in 1983! Amazing. One woman, whose dissertation was on Dickinson in cyberspace (!), said that book, subtitled *Emily Dickinson and the*

Space of the Mind, was especially valuable to her. "More amazing yet," I thought.

Then, last summer, a full professor in his fifties, whom I've known since he was a graduate student, prefaced his remarks by saying that he felt a little nervous speaking in front of so many people who'd been his *mentors*. That felt strange, because we've all grown together, and nobody at our society pulls rank. But it's true: some of us are the most well-known Dickinson scholars in the world. Big fish, small pond. But from my present senior space, these experiences have created an awareness of influence: a term that I'd never really thought about. Influence and legacy: "Suzanne Juhasz" *is* alive.

It helps me to know that my past continues to matter. It gives me a sense of continuity, when I've felt that none existed. Nevertheless, this is now and not then. Now I am trying to find new shoes in which to walk. And write. For the writer is still here: she has morphed rather than vanished. All that I have said about the experience of writing continues, as I choose new forms and subjects, such as this memoir. My writing is now reaching out to a world wider than academia; "Suzanne Juhasz" might come alive in a new way.

PART V

Mapping Senior Space

12

Now: Body and Mind

What does "now" mean, this life as a senior woman, or elder woman, whatever it's called: these years between middle and old age? As this space becomes more populated and even more legitimate in our society, I am not alone in asking these questions. However, though many self-help books aimed at my generation have begun to appear, ultimately, I have to answer it for myself.

To examine "now," I have needed to explore "then." I am not young. I did not arrive here on a parachute. When I look around me and inside me at the experiences that form this time in my life, I continue to have questions, many questions. But I have the support of who I have been before; I have more insights, too.

Then has included my profession, for which I prepared and in which I worked for nearly fifty years. How do I work now? Then has included love from the very beginning: in the family and beyond it. Loving has defined me in profound ways. How do I love now? My body, too, has always been me. How do I live in it now? And finally, what has happened to my good mind? How does it work: as it did before or differently?

I consider these questions by way of a familiar pair of terms: body and mind. They are useful to help me to think about my present identity, for in senior space everything about me seems to have shifted. The aging process is no longer something of which I was peripherally aware but which has become front and center in my life today. It orchestrates how I live and who I am.

My body seems to have become a different place in which to be. It frustrates and often angers me. It no longer gives me joy. But I am different in my mind as well in what seems a more positive, actually fascinating, way. Yes, I have those infamous "senior moments": I forget words and names. I put things in peculiar places. But at the same time, I feel an interesting expansion in my mind. It seems that my view of what there is to see and know has both widened and deepened. I have so much more to go on, as it were: the past assumes a stronger presence in this new world. Memory, working in various ways, helps the past give meaning to the moments that I experience now, even as what happens now shed new light on the past.

Thus, I am at once new and not new, and that may well be the crux of my conundrum.

At first I thought, "How can I be in this body?" Even now, on the few days or even moments that I am without the pain that signals this new state of affairs, I think, "Ah, now I am normal again." But I'm not "normal," because "normal" means back there, where I am not, and I learn this soon enough, when some part of me starts to hurt again. But I'm still surprised, though it's been six years now since arthritis became a major aspect of my life. It had been growing stealthily beforehand, but that one bad fall and its consequences suddenly brought the disease into the foreground. My job is to learn how to live with it, but that isn't easy. I am always working on the problem. Front and center is my therapeutic Pilates instructor, who has given me both strength and understanding of my body. I literally don't know what I would do without her. Then I find caregivers. I have three wonderful women who drive me when I need it, shop, and do errands. They simplify my life, and they have become good friends, as well. But these people cannot help me with figuring out what to do with my body on a daily and even hourly basis. In this life I have to keep my eye on all the parts, all the time.

I understand that "accidents happen," that "the world is never safe." Most importantly, many thousands of human beings live with far greater pain than mine, and they have much more serious problems. However, this is my body, my life, and this is what I have to manage. Friends and family say, "Stop being so timid." "Stop trying to control your environment." "Live!" I agree—tentatively. But not being able to move spontaneously has made me fearful. When does "okay, so it hurts" turn into "this is damage": damage that could worsen one or another body part to the point of needing medical intervention? Each day inevitably brings its share of scary moments, comfortable moments, smaller or larger successes and failures.

Two years ago I had a fall on my way from the bathroom to the bedroom in the middle of the night, which could have had really serious results but thankfully did not: just a badly sprained back from which, my physical therapist says, I recovered much more quickly than most. I say it's because ballet gave me strength and flexibility. So maybe my old body has bequeathed some good things to my new one. Indeed, my Pilates teacher recently said that I ought to have a T-shirt that says, "Resilience." So I think that though I cannot love this body, I can give it some credit: it is trying to help in its own way, a way that ballet taught it.

Still, the body has become so insistent in its pain, its needs for care. "Ignore me at your peril!" it cries. It forces its way into most situations: especially, the ones that matter most, love and work.

The love between me and my daughters, my partner, and my grandchildren is central to me. These relationships are my blessings, but my new body has wrought changes in all of them. I think that my daughters believe my struggle with this disease is exaggerated. I say I won't or I can't do something: something that seems so normal to them that they can't imagine why any ambulant person would make a big deal out of it. Picking up a (to me) heavy item, tying my shoes without a very deep chair to support my back. I've explained to them about the nature of severe arthritis, but I don't seem to get through. Maybe it's because "arthritis" seems so benign, as opposed to so many other chronic diseases. I know it did to me when my doctor first noted its existence in my knee or my back during an examination. "Well, *that*," I thought then. "No big deal." But now it is a big deal.

At first, largely because of my own surprise and distress at my new body, I showed my difficulties all the time. But after I saw the effect of my behavior, I tried to act as if I were just fine. And I tried not to talk about it so much, because this above all else is what other people *do not do*, even senior people. Yet I'm not very good at these things, I know, for my disease occupies so much of my daily experience. I see that my family is leery: I will cause problems, they think. I want to take part. I scope out the chairs in restaurants. (I always bring my trusty Tush Cush to sit on.) I look for the places where the curbs are small or walk to where they're nonexistent. But sometimes I just don't go (and/or they don't ask me).

I feel ashamed, as if I were responsible for this thing that has come between us. Above all, I am ashamed of asking for help. But slowly over these years, I find it sometimes being offered to me. I am so grateful. Yet always I wish for the impossible: that we could return to the days when my body was not an issue but a source of pride for us all.

At home with my partner Branny, who is ten years younger, my frustration grows with my physical dependency. I find it nigh impossible to use the dishwasher or to yank open the dryer door. I have a device to pick up things from the floor, because I can't bend over that well, but many objects (oh, the tyranny of objects) don't respond to the device. Branny will do it, if she's home. Or I just leave it. But often sheer instinct propels me to put out some domestic fire, as when something falls out of the refrigerator so that the door won't close and I put it back, even though I shouldn't bend that far. We have mutuality in our needs, as partners do, for there is much for which she needs me, too. But still, I am not used to such physical dependency. I don't like it.

My family is at the core of my life, but for me living requires work, as well.

I am lucky that writing, my primary passion and skill, is still here for me; that it can take this new turn; and that my body can accomplish it.

Yet there is another side of "now." My body may be diminished, but my mind seems to be working well. In fact, it feels expanded in an interesting way, for by way of the power of memory, the past has become an active agent there. Memories are constant companions, a vital world rather than shadowy figures and events; they occupy a more prominent space there than when I was younger. When they come to the foreground, I frequently like to stop and linger with them. They have added a new dimension to daily life.

But "memory" is too general a term. Memories work in different ways, it turns out, and for different purposes. The most unusual process to me is the way in which present events often seem to be happening in the context of what has gone before, giving a new resonance to the presence. I'm not talking about "living in the past," when nostalgia makes everything there look better. I mean a new kind of perception.

Sometimes people exist for me with our shared pasts like a glow around them. When I am with my daughters, this is naturally most obvious. Jenny and Paul in their forties sit at the dining room table, and I am also taking these two college students to dinner in Providence, at what they think of as a "fancy French restaurant"—a little shack, all the more romantic, on lower Thayer Street. They are newly in love, and the proud mother is celebrating them. They preen before me. Today they have been married for twenty years and are the doting parents of two splendid teenage daughters who fill out their lives, even as once my daughters filled out mine. What I now see is the two of them expanded, moving vigorously in the kind of future that those two young lovers had the capacity to achieve. I am so proud of them, even as I regret that I myself no longer have the power that would make them want the approval that I could bestow upon them that long-ago night in Providence. I am only Grammy, and I am a guest at their table.

With Joseph, my opposite number in the grandparent role, something else can occur. When we talk, and we do talk now, since it's been a long time since we were husband and wife, we are two people who have known one another since *our* teenage years. When I respond to something that he says about his life, or he responds to what I say about mine, our comments are based on so much more than a present dilemma. "You say that you were basically an artist when you were growing up," he says to me, "but you were always the smartest girl in your class. You still are. Don't forget that, as you tell the story of who you are today."

His remarks make me remember places where being the smartest girl in the class in high school didn't always mean feeling gawky and weird, not belonging, as I usually tell it. Places, as only Joseph would remember, like the infamous Benedict Arnold Debating Society (our private name for the that debate club). Or I suddenly think of the year of writing the yearbook: myself and Sheila Ephron as literary editors and diminutive Mrs. Strauss, our faculty advisor—all of us sitting around in her living room of an evening, planning this or that, and drinking cokes from green bottles. In this manner Joseph's comment, fueled by the composite Suzanne/Suzy who he sees across from him, evokes forgotten memories in me that give new insights into my past and consequently how I think of my present self.

Memories, though, are not always this special way of seeing. Another kind of memory is nostalgia. Nostalgia, which is indeed an ingredient in the thinking of older people, gets a bad rap, in that it is generally interpreted as a sentimental romanticization of the past: "How much better it was back then." But there's more to it. Today Facebook thrives on nostalgia, even as at the same time it flaunts a moment-to-moment exploitation of the present. Baby pictures, high-school photos. But Facebook images are fleeting. On the other hand, when I thumb through our old photograph albums, the album itself is a physical part of the past as well as the photographs themselves. I get a thrill from holding that past in my hands and saying, "This was real. The children were that small. I was that young." If this is nostalgia, it connects the past to the present in a positive way.

Especially, memories of events, places, and people that were of particular importance to me then have become significant presences now. An example is the memories of Hillsboro, the summer camp that I attended from the ages of eleven to twenty. It was the best place that I knew.

Of course, summer camps are designed for nostalgia, even when you're young. They're a closed world that exists for a limited amount of time, replete with heightened emotions and an emphasis on rituals, like the little chips of wood on which each of us burned one candle and floated out on the lake on the last night of camp, singing, "This little light of mine / I'm gonna let it shine…" Songs. A song for each cabin, repeated regularly during meals in the dining hall. "We'll sing to Nut House, our only Nut House / The best there is at Hillsboro…" A song for each camper who was leaving with her parents: "Come back, come back, come back, Suzy Hecht, come back, come back…"

Yet for me Hillsboro *did* seem like the real world. At Hillsboro I had years of experience and pleasure producing plays as a drama counselor. But there was so much more. I had friends, I had an exciting emotional and physical life, and I felt that at Hillsboro Suzy Hecht was accepted and loved, something which did not happen at school in Providence. Those weeks at Hillsboro always seemed more real than the outside world, and every year I wept for days when I returned home and could not be there anymore.

Perhaps these memories of Hillsboro are in a separate category from other important memories because they have a particular and special function. When my sister Kathy pointed out to me that there was a Facebook group devoted to our camp, I discovered on it comments from women who had attended it at some period during the last forty years, until it was finally turned into a "family camp." Comments like these: "Our experience there formed us for the rest of our life." "I think of the wonderful years that shaped a lot who I am and why I still cling to these memories." "I am always homesick for Hillsboro." These provide clues to the idea that the creation of self-identity is not always a process limited to a person's earliest years, but that it can be expanded, modified, and even altered throughout a lifetime. There can be new "homes."

At Hillsboro I belonged to a gang of five: Suzy, Chickie, Betsy (Bits, Bets, Chipmunk), Susie, and Judy. The other four were excellent singers (they were in their church choir back in Jackson Heights), so when we five sang together, which was often—walking down the road, sitting in our cabins, and on overnight camping trips—I had to sing the melody, while they could go warbling off into harmony. No matter. I loved the sense of belonging that those close harmonies symbolized. As a group, we moved up through the cabins, getting older every summer, turning into teens, and weaving threads of private jokes and secrets to bind us into a unit of devotion. No wonder Hillsboro felt like the home that I wanted to have.

There are certain people who have mattered so much to me that today it feels as if they exist inside me and participate in my present life. Chick, who was my best friend and drama partner, is one of them. After we grew up, I saw her only occasionally into our twenties, and then we lost touch, apart from an occasional phone call, until finally she lapsed from my present life. But not from my psyche—never. Chickie remained a permanent resident there: my early love, the girl who looked and saw me, even as this recognition was mutual, I believe.

Who was she that she should have meant so much? A skinny girl with large round glasses, a turned-up nose, and a pretty smile. Shy, quiet—that's how everyone saw her and then looked past her. If they did look more carefully, they saw someone odd, a bit strange. But if you knew her, that was a different matter. A gentle soul, truly, a sensitive soul, with a searching mind. And when she was happy and relaxed, there was a wild sense of humor, and out came that boisterous laugh. Odd? Strange? Yes, she was. But these were virtues. There was no one like her: her perceptions were unique, and I had the key to her. We wrote many camp songs together, some of which became fixtures in the Hillsboro repertoire. We shared our tastes in books and music. From her I learned about old English folk songs and Alfred Dyer Bennett. I introduced her to Noël Coward. We thought of ourselves as artistic, clever, and sophisticated. When we were apart each year, we wrote pages of letters on lavender stationery, sharing every idea, experience, and dream. Perfect trust had developed between us over all those summers.

When Kathy introduced me to the Hillsboro Facebook page, to my delight there was another of the five friends: Betsy! Soon we were emailing. She was as eager to find me, as I was to find her. Betsy turned out to be the same in the most essential ways: clever, wisecracking, and smart. What a treat to know her now. And then suddenly, Betsy had news of Chick! Bad news, actually, but even so, Chick. She was suffering from early-onset dementia. I wrote her, understanding that that she'd never answer. Through Betsy, I followed her downhill slide. Finally, she was placed in a nursing home: I sent her a birthday card there. This spring she died.

The shock was enormous, and the grief was deep. How could I be so jarred, when I hadn't seen her in fifty years? The circumstances of her later years, as Betsy recounted them, were so sad and unhappy; her early death seemed so wrong. That was part of it, surely. But I think that it had been somehow comforting all of my life to know that though she may have been in my heart, she was as well out there, living her life, always knowing me as I knew her, even if what we'd had was an adolescent and then young womanhood friendship. That feeling was brutally severed. Now, after the shock of death has quieted, I understand that she still remains with me as always, everything who she was in our growing years forever with me. Nonetheless, she is lost to life. To say that a bit of me is gone is such a cliché, but it's true. And so I hurt for her, and I hurt for myself.

Chick was one of the people who developed my sense of identity. Another is Josephine Miles, my mentor and graduate advisor at Berkeley. Like Chick, her presence has been ongoing not just as my partner in writing but in other ways, too.

At Berkeley the professors amazed me, as they worked out their ideas before me. The level of what they did was nothing like what I had encountered before in its depth and sometimes elegance. However, it was not until I met the famous Miss Miles that my life turned around forever.

I think that Jo Miles was a second mother to me, different from my biological mother because she recognized me for myself. She chose me, helping me to learn who that self was and might become. As she nurtured me for our years together, she became a part of me, as I understand it. Once, when as a young scholar, I asked her awkwardly for yet another letter of reference. She replied, "Once I take a student, I take you for life." My life, not only hers.

I went to see Miss Miles in her office a few weeks before the beginning of the Fall Semester of my first year as a PhD student. I had passed those nasty MA orals on my second try. I wanted to study metaphor, and I was told that she was the person to ask, an expert on poetic language. That week Joseph was away in New York, and I had a two-month-old baby, so little Jenny came with me in a pink plastic baby seat, which I placed on the desk between us, as there was nowhere else to put it. Not an auspicious way to begin my interview with this revered professor, famous for, among other things, her supposed dislike of women (not true, as a matter of fact). But what could I do?

I had never seen her. Now before me sat a wizened little woman with a skin as hard as a nut, and her dark eyes were lively with intelligence. She *liked* the baby, so I heaved a sigh of relief, but we got down to business right away. I wanted to do an independent study with her on metaphor and poetry. First, she asked me about metaphor: Why did I like it and what did I think it was? I answered to the best of my ability. What poets did I like who used metaphor? I thought hard. "Dylan Thomas?" I proffered. Not so good, it seemed. Did I know anything about William Carlos Williams? she asked. I blanched. I'd never heard of him. I had to tell her that.

"Good," she said. "I don't know much about him either. But he's growing quite popular these days, though he hasn't had much scholarly notice. You can help me find out more." She added, "And you won't be biased, one way or the other. Why don't you go home and write me a short paper on metaphor in Williams over the weekend?"

Yikes! Joseph gone, me with a baby and a three-year-old, and this? But I sat down in the next few days and did it. I showed up in her office on Monday.

After she read it, she said, "I think that you should take my seminar this fall." It was on eighteenth-century poetic theory.

I said, "Couldn't we do an independent study?"

She replied, "Oh, I always think that people learn better with more than one mind to bounce off. You'd be bored with just me." But then she added, "Later we can work on metaphor."

This was so very Jo Miles, but I didn't understand it then. That she had accepted me at all—first in asking me to write the paper and then in taking me into her seminar. These were privileges, not givens. That she imagined a future with me was a very big deal. Over the years I learned that she truly respected her students: she really did think that I might help her to learn something. Finally, the challenge of that first assignment was not to show that she was a scary professor but to throw me into deep waters to see if I could swim: if I would accept later challenges to my assumptions and my skills.

I took two classes with her, and then <u>she</u> asked <u>me</u> if I would write my dissertation with her. You had to be chosen to work with Professor Miles and not the other way around. It wasn't that she was a snob—she was not—but that she wanted to work with someone whom she could challenge and who would challenge her so that something good could come of it.

The wizened face and the leathery skin, the leg that did not move, and the claw-like hands were the result of childhood arthritis. As a girl she had been carried into her classrooms on a wooden plank. But she healed enough to walk by herself for brief stretches, although she moved that leg from the hip, to go to college and then graduate school at UCLA and then to become a professor at Cal, as Berkeley was called. When I knew her, she always had a driver for her little Volkswagen, a young man who could carry her (she was so small), but she walked into a classroom by herself, every time. She wrote her incisive comments with a pencil with those misshapen hands.

She was a stickler for discipline, for assignments and papers done on time. No extensions were allowed. "Monday's paper is not Friday's paper," she'd say. And, "There is always a time to read and a time to write." Once she overheard me when I was telling a classmate about my little daughter's bout with pneumonia and the tent around her bed in the hospital. Later she said to me, "I was so sorry to hear about your daughter and am glad that she is better now." But the paper was due when the paper was due. How could anyone dispute this, after what she had done to become Professor Miles?

And so I entered the heady world of Miss Miles: her brilliance, her kindness, her standards, her generosity. Little Suzy Juhasz, who thought she was so smart (and who was so insecure), grew up to be an intellectual under this wise and also witty tutelage. Jo took me and my whole family under her wing, as I made my way through the stages of my PhD degree: the oral examination, thesis tutorials, the prospective exam, and finally the writing of my dissertation.

Jo in her chair in her North Berkeley home, a board across her lap for writing, a speaker phone so that she could converse with her many friends. I would walk to her little house on Virginia Street from my apartment lower down the hill, holding my latest offering: a proposal or a chapter. Or I would be going there to receive her response to last week's writing. But always with the same excitement and anticipation. I'd settle into my seat on her couch, and we would begin. She never disappointed. There was always something unexpected in what she had to say. Even though I'd work so hard to get it right and never did, at least not right away, her comments seemed worth the price, nudging me in a new direction, a place that I hadn't considered. Her comments were never harsh, like those from so many of my Berkeley professors. That was not her style. She prompted; she didn't seem to judge. We were comrades now. And when she liked it, wow. I knew that I'd done something real, something of which to be proud. Those years were an education in more than literary criticism: she taught me how to think.

After I received my PhD in 1970, she and I were in contact for many years. I always visited when I went to Berkeley, and we wrote to one another. I cherish the few postcards and letters that I still have. They are responses to my books, my poetry, and my life, as I struggled to find work in the profession. Here is one snippet of Milesian advice: "Don't you sometimes feel that you are digging up your plants to see if they are growing?" Ah, too true of me then and always.

I wrote an essay about her, "Style and Proportion: Josephine Miles as Example." Also, I told many stories about her in my classes, for they helped me to teach students truths of which they were never aware. Teaching her wisdom was a threefold pleasure: it gave the student important knowledge; it gave me the joy of hearing her voice, as I spoke her words, and it made her teaching a living presence in a world from which she was gone.

She died in 1985 when I was in my thirties.

Like Chickie Williams, Jo Miles has stayed with me always, but it is only now that I am so aware of the continuing presence of the past that I understand the profound importance of these two women. Each in her own way was formative for me, for by recognizing me each became a part of my very identity.

Body and mind create the whole person. What seems most obvious as I look at these aspects of myself is change. I have wrinkles on my skin; I have Medicare for health insurance; I am retired. Who am I? It seems that I am still Suzanne, who persists as these changes occur. However, the changes matter, too.

I began this book because this stage of my life seems both especially important and especially complicated. I am that much closer to inevitable death, I understand, but I do not feel at the doorstep yet, although of course that is something I cannot know. But now the future no longer stretches out in a seemingly endless way. There is not much time to wander, to say, "Well, if this doesn't work out, something else will." Others feel differently on this matter, I know, but for me "now" is not the time to "rest on my laurels." I have to live to my *full*est capacity in whatever way that I can. To do this, I need to understand of what I am capable and where my gifts now lie. I want to feel worthwhile, and I want to give something of value to my family and to the world beyond.

This is why the question of identity comes so dramatically to the fore. Social roles—daughter, wife, mother, student, professor—have helped to define me, but within these outlines, as I have shown, there is much mobility, not to mention the fact that some of them persist and some do not, and sometimes new roles arise.

With respect to my body, I can simply say that mine no longer gives me pleasure. What I have called my corporeal self is different from before, and this has strongly affected me and others with whom I come into contact. Nevertheless, I am not seriously ill and do not have to deal with that sort of problem at this time. I am lucky in the general state of things, and this is a gift that I have right now.

Another gift is that I have is my good mind. My life as a thinker and a writer has always contributed enormously to my sense of self. But only recently have I realized that there is more to this gift: I am a writer! Well, of course I'm a writer. I've always been a writer. But I suddenly understand that I'm not a writer like I was before. It's not just the subject matter that is different or even the form that it takes. It's the place that writing holds in my life.

I always envied the people whom I thought of as real writers. Novelists, poets, essayists: those people. My work as a professor of English was to write *about* them and teach about them. But they write for a living. They wake up every day and sit at their typewriter—now computer—and put in their hours. Writing is what they do. Writing is their profession. And now it is mine.

Nevertheless, my new profession has meant that my position vis-à-vis the world at large has changed considerably. I am not a public person anymore in my daily life. It seems strange and at the same time pleasant. I am used to selecting my clothes and accessories every day and going out there. I like being looked at, but it makes me anxious, too. I was often laughed at when I was young, and I never really got over that, no matter how many successes I had. I like not having to prove myself in public all the time, which is another reason why I slithered out of the theatre scene. And I like being freer from the constant pressure of meeting deadlines, which translates into another version of proving myself. (Yes, publication is another form of public, but the audience meets the book, not the writer.)

There's another important aspect to my current life as a writer. I've found that moving from academic writing to trade writing is not as simple as I'd imagined: it's actually changing careers. The writing style is different, of course, but more different yet is the publishing process, which has little in common with what I know from working with university presses all these years. Even the vocabulary is different. What is a "platform"? I didn't know. I was looking for something new, but I didn't think that I'd find it here.

In the family what is most obvious is that I am more peripheral, both as a mother and a grandmother. As a mother, I now have middle-aged adult daughters. Two are now mothers themselves. My daughters run the family now. As a grandmother, I am neither that cookie-baking lady nor even sought after as a companion these days, though I do host good afternoon teas. I am not the wise old woman to whom everyone turns for counsel, a role that grandmothers sometimes have. I am wise enough, I think, but they don't seem to have need of one. So although I still wake every morning as I have done for fifty years and tick off in my head where my daughters—and now my grandchildren— are and how they are doing, my involvement in their daily lives is minor, for that's what they need and want. The bottom line is that I need these girls more than they need me. But perhaps just knowing that they have my unconditional love helps a little to give them their independence.

The upside of my situation is that I have this wonderful family. They are delightful, smart, beautiful people, every one. We remain a tight clan, and I am so lucky for that. I try to accept my new position in my family and use it well.

Six years after retirement, I am still in transition, trying to come to terms with what I have and don't have—what I've done and haven't done. I don't feel that I have reached all my goals, but on the other hand, I have achieved some valuable things in this altered space and time, and I can keep trying.

Arriving in senior space has felt like an explosion, but perhaps it is more like a sea change. Writing these chapters, I see all the Suzannes, so am I not still Suzanne right now, even when I often feel so different from her? Is there not a kind of stability in the knowledge of mutability? Do I have something like a core self, even as I've played a variety of roles throughout the years? When I was trying to figure out how high to put the blanket on baby Alexandra's sleeping little body, or when my heart was wrenching with grief as she set off for college, or when I was watching her sing her baby Gabriel to sleep— are not all those Suzannes still me? Or when I was Suzy Hecht in high school, writing dramatic poems about dinosaurs (it's true); was a young feminist, writing soul-baring poems about all my relationships; and was a scholar, writing essays on Emily Dickinson?

But at the same time, my present feeling of instability is also real and oughtn't to be dismissed. A lifelong tendency of mine may help to explain my trouble at present: my way of arranging my life so that it will work for me. I need routine. Routine makes me feel safe. When changes occur—large or small—I am disturbed and worried, especially when people leave. For me "now" is a big change, a very big one.

Still, I should add that some of the changes have been created by me. I am always striving for something better. Throughout my life, I have left situations—and people—behind because I thought that they weren't right. (I called this "folding up my tent.") For example, I was the one who caused the retirement to occur early. I may well be responding to this new life stage in a way that is typical of being me, rather than a moment where I have lost myself.

I used to talk about Emily Dickinson's poems as like snowballs. What I meant was this. Her poems are rarely linear stories: and then and then and then. In her opening line or two, she sets out a proposition, an idea, or a question. Then her stanzas proceed by way of comparison or parallelism, where new thoughts, usually expressed obliquely by way of metaphors or similes, add on to the meaning of the first thought, each time enriching it, making it more complex and often more perplexing. But they always refer back to the beginning of the poem. Thus the snowball effect: starting as a little ball, rolling along through the snow and getting fatter. So my selfhood. Rolling along through time, adding on more experiences, so that things get more complex (and sometimes perplexing), but staying at heart much the same. This is what some psychologists call the core self. (Other psychologists don't believe that one exists—but I do.)

Now is where my particular snowball has arrived: not yet old, but getting old. "Who am I?" I continue to ask. Is this question the first line of my poem (life), to push the Dickinson analogy a little further? "Now" is one stanza of this poem. Each day in this space, senior space, contributes moments that are good, sad, scary, confusing, satisfying, or even beautiful. I try to notice this, even as I continue to imagine a place for myself where I feel more settled and thus stronger, more effective. "Now" continues to seem unstable. But since I've been here for a while, and I haven't fallen off the edge, I can see how the sense of challenge that I experience is as much a part of it as the vertigo.

When I sing, I've felt the past and the present overlapping. When I write about the past from the present moment, the same thing happens over a much longer period of time: I sense that I inhabit both. Feeling the presence of the past is a boon for a person in senior space, for it helps to make a life seem whole albeit complex. Instead of hanging on by a thread, I am adding to the pattern that the strands of my life are weaving. I am not on a tightrope, as I sometimes feel, but rather experiencing my place in the fabric that is still forming.

Acknowledgements

I would like to thank those people who have given me support and aid during the process of bringing this book to completion. First, thank you to my family, to the four generations whom I have known. They are my foundation, and each in her or his own way has enriched my life. Special thanks to my partner Branny, who has been steadfast in her belief in me and this book and whose perceptive suggestions at key moments have contributed to my work. I thank the very first readers of a tentative manuscript for their encouragement and advice: my cousin Judith Kolb Morris, who has known me all of my life and who is a smart and passionate reader; my friend Martha Ackmann, who brought her experience in the worlds of both trade publishing and academic publishing to her evaluation and suggestions. Deep gratitude goes to my editor, Anne Dubuisson, who encountered my manuscript at a critical later stage, for her consummate skill: her insight, precision, and creativity. No idea or word escaped her discerning eye, as she worked with me on the manuscript. She has been the editor of whom every writer dreams, as we brought this book to its present form together. She has enhanced my life as well as my writing.

About The Author

Suzanne Juhasz is a retired professor of English and women's studies from the University of Colorado, Boulder. She has a BA in creative writing and theater from Bennington College and earned her MA and PhD degrees in English from the University of California at Berkeley.

In addition to her memoir, Juhasz has written nine other books, including *The Undiscovered Continent: Emily Dickinson and the Space of the Mind* and *Reading from the Heart: Women, Literature, and the Search for Romance*. She has published numerous essays, most recently "Classroom Ballerina: The Sequel," in *Persimmon Tree, An Online Magazine of the Arts for Women Over Sixty*, as well as poetry and short stories. In 1998, she received the Distinguished Senior Scholar Award from the American Association of University Women.

Suzanne Juhasz lives in Boulder, Colorado, with her partner. She is a proud mother and grandmother.

94902040R00155

Made in the USA
Columbia, SC
04 May 2018